Deliberate Acts of Random

by
Jon Nikrich

Table of Contents

Introduction 1

The Introverted Dead 3

A Ninja Obsession Phase 7

Apocalypse Now-ish... 15

A Short Conversation... 55

A Whole Other Sinister Level 57

The British are Visiting... 63

Brotherly Love 75

Dodos... 135

And Eric Bana 136

The Stubborns 140

Very 152

Bad Bet... 154

Duck.. 164

Better than Santa... 165

What I Did When I Wasn't Saving the World (Prologue) ...171

What I Did When I Wasn't Saving the World (Part 1).......178

What I Did When I Wasn't Saving the World (Part 2).......199

What I Did When I Wasn't Saving the World (Part 3).......273

The Clock Tower... 315

Spheres of Creepy Influence 316

Acknowledgements 323

Introduction

I set out to write something akin to a collection of stories from different collaborators, only with me as all the collaborators. The inconsistent styles, approaches and themes throughout the book are deliberate and made possible by my inconsistent psychological state. You are welcome to draw conclusions about my psychological state.

Everything that follows is fictional, except for what isn't. None of the characters are based on anyone I know, except for the ones who are based on people I know. Most of the people on whom I've based characters know that they are the people on whom I've based characters.

None of the events in this book are true, except for the events that really happened, including the events that happened to me. All of the opinions expressed are those of fictional characters and do not reflect my own opinions, except for the opinions about movies, my own face and Santa.

I would like to offer a sincere and grateful thank you to everyone who assisted with this and my previous publications. Please don't draw conclusions about their psychological states. That would be mean.

The Introverted Dead

A very short story.

The archway and the old wall that connected to each side of it were all that persisted. Nothing remained of the demolished church, a building that had collapsed centuries earlier and of which no complete images survived. The rectangle enclosed by the redundant wall, the space in which the church and its graveyard had once resided, belonged to him and his kind.

He haunted the ground, the earth below, the air above and every misshapen, diseased tree that littered it. The path on the other side of the arch belonged to The Widow. She allowed him to scare anyone who attempted the short journey through his domain. Recently he'd allowed people to pass safely into her realm. He hoped their passage would draw her. He hoped that he might glimpse her.

The six teenagers, three pretty girls, three overconfident boys, passed him safely, obliviously, as they crossed the former graveyard. He watched them walk under the stone archway and through the gate. They were now at The Widow's mercy until they reached the road on the western edge of the old wood.

He could have warned the visitors, but he never considered it for a moment. This was the ghostly equivalent of live sport. Jay was the crowd, five years dead and cheering for the home team.

The Widow appeared above them, hidden by a network of branches, no more than a ghostly presence. The youths walked on, blind to her intentions. Jay saw it immediately because he knew what to look for. Her approach was perfect. He almost applauded.

The Widow looked at him and their eyes met. Her glance fell and her mood darkened. She jabbed three times in his direction with her index finger.

You. Yes, you. Stay there.

He smiled the geeky smile of an enthusiastic fan and pointed at himself three times.

Me. Yes, me. I'm staying here.

Jay's best friend George appeared behind Jay's shoulder and her expression fell further. She jabbed her finger in the air towards him. George interrupted her gesture with an upheld, open palm. He nodded that he understood.

The Widow whispered something to herself. George couldn't lip read, but it appeared to be a variation on 'I'm trying to work here'. She hated performing for an audience.

"What are you doing?" George whispered to Jay.

"I'm just, you know, watching her in action. Did you hear that last group scream?"

Jay returned his attention to current events, realized that George's attention remained on him and turned back to face his friend.

"What?"

"You like her."

"No, I don't. ... OK, yes, I do, but I don't *like her* like her. I ... admire her technical abilities."

"You should talk to her."

"You think I should? No. What would I say? We don't have anything in common. ... OK. Yes. We have something in common, but it's not a great line, is it? 'So, hey, I'm dead, you're dead, how's that working out for you?'"

"You're right. You should go with 'I admire your technical abilities.'"

"You're no help."

"Who said I'm helping? Pointing out the flaws in your every thought process is the only fun I have anymore."

They paused as two of the teenage girls complained nervously that they didn't like this part of the wood. The boys in the group laughed at their expense. Jay and Joy laughed quietly at the boys.

"What do you want to do tonight?" Jay whispered. "Do you want to scare somebody?"

"While she's in a zone? It would be embarrassing. She's world class. We're amateur hour by comparison."

"So, you admit she's something special?"

"Yeah, she's something special. I still think you should talk to her."

"... Maybe tomorrow night. She's on a roll right now. It wouldn't be fair."

"You're going to stall until after Halloween, aren't you?"

"It's only considerate. This is a key month for her."

"Yeah, but I know you. Next week, you'll think of another reason and ... You already have an excuse for next week, don't you?"

"... I am a little concerned about age difference. ... But, look, we haunt neighbouring parts of a really creepy wood. I've got eternity to work up the courage."

"Watching you mess this up is going to be painful."

The Widow floated gently to the ground and hid herself close to the nearest teenager, with only a tree to hide her patient pursuit.

"Look at the way she closed in on this group." Jay said, impressed. "Did you see the way she cycled around for the guy who fell behind."

"It's true." George admitted. "You have to admire her technical abilities."

A Ninja Obsession Phase

A short story. Based on an idea by Daniel, age 7.

He hesitated on the sidewalk. It looked like a school. More than that, it looked a lot like half the schools he had visited in the previous week. Despite this, part of him feared he was the victim of an elaborate hoax.

He slid a piece of paper from his pocket and checked the address. He quickly cross-referenced it with what he remembered from the web site. As he did so, smartly-dressed, well-behaved students passed by him and entered through the building's doors.

He followed them into a hallway and found the main office. In his momentary confusion, he selected a word from his European childhood.

"I'd like to speak to the headmaster."

The receptionist stared back, confused, and he realized his mistake.

"Sorry, I mean the principal. I'm here to see the principal. My son is a prospective student."

"Oh, you're here to see Sensei Max." she said. "He's expecting you. He'll be here shortly."

She invited him to sit in a nearby seat. More students arrived and he realized what had troubled him since entering the building. It was too quiet. It looked like a school, but it didn't sound like one. He watched the teenagers walk on unimaginatively tiled floors alongside impressive student art.

He noticed a plaque. It read "School Mantra – Education may save your life someday."

A middle aged man approached. He was slightly overweight and slightly balding. His clothes were smart and professional. The new arrival knew who his visitor was prior to any introductions.

"I'm so glad you decided to visit." the principal said. "I could tell you about our school over the phone, but it will be so much more persuasive to show you."

"The receptionist told me your name was ... she said ..."

"Please, call me Max. I find principal too formal and some of the alternatives are inaccurate and embarrassing. Follow me and I'll show you what we do here."

They walked down the nearest hallway and the principal launched into his sales pitch.

"As you know, the city's board of education manages a large number of schools. Many of them use traditional techniques and models, and they adopt a similar approach to each other. However, the school board also offers a selection of specialist schools that cater to a particular type of student. There are boys-only schools, girls-only schools, science academies, technical colleges, creative arts programs and language immersions. Each customizes the student experience for a particular type of child. We do the same. For a certain kind of student, we're a dream come true."

The man coughed and summoned the courage to ask the obvious question.

"So, your website is … I mean, I knew that the school board supported specialized institutions for arts, sciences and languages. I wasn't aware of the … ninja program until earlier this week."

"Yes, we're fairly unique. We're the only one in Canada that I am aware of and there are only, I believe, three in the United States. But I think we're a valuable alternative for a certain type of individual."

"What kind of individual is that?"

"What kind of individual is your teenager?"

"He's lacking a clear career focus and he's temporarily delusional."

"Yes, I think delusion explains most of our student population. It may be why all of our student population is male too."

They approached some heavy wooden doors. The principal opened the left of the two doors and they entered into a sports hall adorned with a complex network of climbing equipment.

A plaque on the far wall read "School Mantra – Thinking on your feet starts with thinking."

"We're very happy with our gymnasium." the principal said. "In keeping with our mandate, we have less of a focus on team games. Instead, we concentrate on balance, upper body strength, stamina and gymnastics. We also do a lot of running; if you're going to be a ninja and you're not a particularly good one, you need to be good at running."

As he finished his sentence, a student launched himself from one collection of beams to another and landed expertly. The guest's jaw dropped and the principal smiled proudly. He led his visitor back out of the room.

"Tell me more about your son."

"For one thing, he's Caucasian. Is that an issue?"

"No. Most of our students are. We find that most of the ethnicities that experience, for want of a better term, a ninja obsession phase, experience it at about age seven. It's mostly Caucasians who drift into it in their early to mid-teens."

"I didn't realize it was such a common issue."

"It's more common than you'd think. And the enthusiasm and drive it generates is something we can work with, particularly in students that haven't demonstrated much enthusiasm or drive before. However, I freely admit that the success we guarantee is not necessarily the success they seek."

"What do you mean?"

"The ninja industry is extremely competitive. The elite ninjas, its top earners, are not typically the ones who settled on ninja as a future career in their mid-teens. Most of the industry's highest earning professionals are the ones following in family footsteps. Many of the others were forcibly conscripted and started their training at age five.

That's a tremendous head start and it can be tough to compete with."

They hesitated near some classrooms and the parent glanced through the open doorway. The room's equipment was first class and the attentive students were spellbound.

"I wondered how that would work." the parent whispered. "You're a school for ninjas whose students don't become ninjas."

"Yes, in most cases, ninja is the teaching strategy and not the eventual career. Our official goal is to guide any child with whom we are entrusted on a journey to become a skilled and fearsome master of shadows. Our unofficial goal is to provide a valuable education that will benefit each student whatever his eventual career destination. And our track record is impeccable."

"What do you mean?"

"We don't educate only, we transform. We've helped a wide variety of students and achieved this under the umbrella of a ninja education. We can calm calamitous fashion sense and dissuade compulsive interruption. We can eliminate clumsiness. We encourage the smelly to wash and the practical jokers to refrain. There really is no limit to our potential influence."

"You take everything that makes a teenage boy and you un-teenage them?"

"We even persuade them to discard squeaky shoes. It is also important to note that we customize our response to each individual child and we do so in such a way that the student chooses to do these things. We enforce little. All of this is essential because, let's be honest, teenager and ninja are almost antonyms."

"What about their formal education? Can you tell me about the syllabus?"

"We cover all the core subjects and all the learning objectives that the school board insists on. However, we customize the lessons with the inclusion of alternative examples and additional readings to make everything more ninja-focused. We teach project management disguised as covert mission planning. We teach shuriken trajectories in math. We teach communication and language skills, but recast them as espionage. You get the idea. In addition, as you can see, we have state of the art facilities that help us eradicate the most common, least ninja-like traits."

They drifted away from the classrooms. As they did so, the parent spotted a plaque on the wall.

It read "School Mantra - Hard work of the right kind in the right way at the right time is your best chance to achieve your dreams."

"I notice that you have more than one mantra."

"Yes, we have many." the principal replied. "With an unconventional institution such as ours, I don't think it's possible to over-mantra."

They turned a corner and found themselves opposite the cafeteria. The students inside were snacking on salads, fruit and vegetables.

"Teenagers in general don't enjoy a good diet. We have more success than most schools because we frame personal health as an essential element of their future career."

"I don't think my son would like that."

"You'd be surprised. We have junk food options, but the peer pressure typically steers students towards healthy choices faster than anything we could tell them."

"Part of me can't believe what I am seeing."

"I know. That's a frequent response. Yet, you're seeing it."

The principal led him around another corner and they entered into a welcoming, open-plan library. It hosted all of the usual areas, but sported an additional, well-stocked ninja section that seemed to magnetically draw the younger students.

A plaque on the wall read "School Mantra - Knowledge is a weapon you can carry with you everywhere."

"The receptionist at the front desk called you Sensei Max. Do you have a martial arts background?"

"No, the title is honorary. My background is actually educational theory. However, I have two years as the principal for a school that teaches its students deception and stealth. That keeps you on your toes and I believe I've picked up a few tips."

They exited through a non-descript door and arrived in the car park near to the visitor's vehicle.

"I hope you enjoyed the tour. If you have any questions, e-mail the school and we'll answer any that we can. That said, I already sense we may be the right place for your son."

The parent nodded.

"You may be. You really may be."

The two men paused and looked back at the remarkable facility.

"I know what you're thinking." the principal added. "You're wishing that the school had existed when you were a teenager."

The parent stared at him wide-eyed. After the wonders he'd recently observed, he instinctively suspected some form of telepathy.

"How could you possibly know that?"

"I was thinking the same thing," the principal explained, "the exact same thing."

Apocalypse Now-ish

A short story.

"I don't want to argue." I said. "We could all die tomorrow."

"We won't die tomorrow." Cate replied.

"You don't know that."

"Yes, I do. Beth, help me with the calculations. What are you thinking?"

Beth completed the complex analysis in her head.

"A couple of blocks, standard rate of progress ... we could all die Thursday."

"There you go. We won't die tomorrow. It's Thursday at the earliest."

I took a deep breath.

"Cate, I don't want to argue. We could all die on Thursday."

"Yeah, OK. Point taken."

I wish I could tell you that this debate was unusual. The truth is that we argue about death a lot. This happens when the odds of its occurrence increase as greatly as it has for us.

All the same, I hate our arguments. I've only known Cate for eight weeks, but in that time I've come to regard her as a sister. When you've lost as much as we have, you don't want to argue with family.

My name is Esther. Cate, Beth and I are children of catastrophe, survivors of the end of the world. The only good news, effectively hidden among all of the bad, is that the messengers of the Armageddon are slower than you might expect.

It started with an airborne virus. Either you were immune or infected, and by infected I mean a rapid deterioration into a vicious, mindless shell. The immune became the infected's favourite target.

It's not really a zombie apocalypse and what we're dealing with aren't really zombies. However, everyone who could correct us in our misuse of terminology has turned into something that isn't truly a zombie and we accept this as permission to use whatever terminology we want.

There are several differences between the infected and your traditional movie zombie. The most notable is their walking pace. These are not the rage monsters of 28 Days Later. These are not even the shambling creatures of early Romero. These are a whole other speed bracket, as if each and every step requires their careful consideration.

It is due to their restricted mobility that I progressed from shock to terror to fear and finally to matter of fact acceptance. I understood that we'd somehow survived a terrible disaster. I knew we roamed a deserted cityscape. Yet, our mortal enemy, our nemesis in a realm we no longer ruled, boasted the hunting pace of a snail.

We face life-threatening situations weekly, but we typically receive three or four days to plan our response. It's not fun to battle for your life, but the rate of each battle's approach is convenient and strangely considerate.

In the early days of the crisis, almost everyone fled from the cities. They inadvertently took most of the crisis with them. We stayed because we had nowhere obvious to go. We dodged the worst of the disaster and we inherited an abandoned city as our personal playground.

I didn't see anyone for the first week. After gaining an appreciation for how the zombies struggled with staircases, I moved to one of the higher floors in The Sheraton near the river.

My new home had everything I needed except for everything it lacked, which by no coincidence was what everywhere lacked. It was as safe as anywhere else I had tried. It was comfortable. It felt more like a home than my other available options, including my actual home. My relocation strategy clearly had merit because more women arrived within days of my arrival. They each selected rooms and we spread across floors 8, 9 and 10.

I can't explain why my millennial comrades and I outlasted the boomers, the Xers and the Gen Ys. All of us were independent. All of us were based in the city centre and boasted excellent knowledge of classic horror movies. Make of that what you will.

These women are my family now and this is our city.

Cate announced a meeting and we gathered in a neutral room on the tenth floor we'd adopted as the base for impromptu discussions. I was the last to arrive because I had the furthest to walk.

The six of us selected somewhere to sit. I sat on the edge of a bed near to Gin, a tiny blonde who looked like an unlikely survival candidate. She was shy and fragile. She was also the reason for my argument with Cate.

Whenever we ventured out for supplies, one of us stayed behind to guard our possessions. We shared this task between the group, but I wanted the responsibility to skip past Gin. In the event of a problem at the Sheraton, Gin would be useless as our champion. She would provide no protection and might only succeed in getting hurt. Cate believed it was important that each of us share the workload, regardless of size and strength. We failed to find a compromise.

On the room's other bed, their backs against the walls and their long legs stretched in front of them, were Kelly and Jess. They were prettier than me and they dedicated much of their available time to ensuring that the end of the world didn't interfere with their attractive appearance.

Cate stood near the window with Beth. Cate was the fastest, the strongest and the bravest of us, which is why we had selected her as our leader before she'd had a chance to nominate herself. Beth was more intelligent than the rest of us put together. She's so smart that nobody understood her when she explained her pre-crisis career.

I feared Cate had called the meeting to bring our argument to a wider audience. Independent of my hatred for our confrontations, my dissension was foolish. When Cate spoke, we all listened, and the others would side with her nine times out of ten.

As I discovered, she had different news to share.

"There's a horde on the way." Gin whispered, louder than she intended, spoiling the surprise.

"It's not a horde." Cate corrected.

"You've seen it?" I asked.

"I've seen it. It's not a horde. It's a … I don't know. What's the collective name for a small group of zombies?"

"A shamble?" Kelly suggested. "A moan? Oh, how about a rot?"

"I thought it was horde." Jess added.

"It's not a horde." Cate said. "Horde implies something bigger."

"It is kind of horde-ish." Beth agreed.

Cate cast a dirty look.

"I'm sorry," Beth said. "but I've seen it too and it does have horde-like qualities."

"How about a pack?" I suggested.

Cate pointed at me.

"Thank you, yes, it's not a horde. It's only a pack."

She paused and let the information sink in.

"What do we need to do?" I asked.

"We watch them. We monitor their approach. If their numbers increase, we may need to move."

Her conclusion was unpopular but predictable. We liked our home, but we knew that nothing in this life was permanent or completely safe. That included the places. That included the people. We'd learned that lesson the hard way by losing the seventh member of our group.

Later in the same meeting, Cate announced that we needed more supplies and that Gin would be taking her turn as the hotel's protector. She presented it as a decision, not the start of a discussion. She looked at me as she said it and I didn't argue.

"Zombie" Beth said.

Our eyes drifted to where she had seen it, a doorway fifteen feet from our route. It completed a single step towards us. In unrehearsed, synchronised harmony, we each took a sideways step away from it. It didn't affect our pace. It barely dented our conversation.

"What are we thinking today?" Cate asked.

"Residential." I replied. "We need food."

"Residential is more dangerous." Kelly complained in a less-than-secret code that we all understood.

She wanted the group to split so that she could raid clothes stores while we simultaneously secured her next meal.

Scavenging as a group was a new strategy. Previously, we'd set out individually or in pairs. That policy had changed quickly after Nora had gone looking for a headache tablet and never returned. She's the only person we've lost since our arrival at the hotel. In some ways, I'm more upset about losing Nora than I am about losing everyone else.

"We stay together." Cate said and the conversation ended.

We never argue with Cate. We're a team and she's the leader. She wants to keep everyone safe even more than I do.

"We'll look at clothes first," Cate continued. "but everyone carries what they steal and nobody carries for anyone else. We're not attempting a food hunt with Kelly's autumn wardrobe in our arms."

We agreed to the compromise.

Each time we ventured out on a supplies run, our main targets were food and medicine, but we reserved the right to let bargains distract us. We're easily distracted, some more than others. And we live in an abandoned city, so there are a lot of bargains. That makes us happy, even when we can't find food and medicine, which is more often than we'd like.

Our frequent acquisition of new clothes may seem superficial. Maybe we are, but I would suggest that there is a deeper motive behind our shallow considerations. It's a welcome change in our conversation. It's something within our power to achieve, from a list of possibilities that shortens daily. I can't underestimate the importance of alternate goals, because the day we give up, we're doomed.

"Zombie." Beth said.

We glanced sideways and saw it watch us from the shadows. We completed our subliminal, coordinated sidestep and continued our journey.

We selected the nearest department store. Jess and Kelly disappeared in the direction of the women's section without awaiting Cate's signal. Cate sighed and set off after them, assuming that they would benefit from her protection more than Beth and I.

I went in search of the men's department, hoping to secure some new jeans, boots and t-shirts. As far back as I can remember, half my wardrobe has been men's clothing. There was something comforting about maintaining that tradition. Beth came with me, not because she felt the same way about clothes, but because she wanted a short break from Kelly and Jess.

We ascended the steps as quietly as possible. Listening is one of the most valuable resources at our disposal. As a self-preservation strategy, it resides near the top of the list, along with drifting wide around corners and selecting the widest paths. As a weapon, it rivals baseball bats and golf clubs. We can solve problems if we need to. It's easier when we don't need to.

We secured clothes for ourselves first, an easy score from a wide selection. I spent longer selecting new boots because I wanted a pair that would fit me immediately and not require a painful, breaking-in period. I picked out a few, small items for Gin that I thought might fit her, but I was guessing. I'd forgotten to ask her size.

"Oh no." Beth said.

"What oh no?"

"What's as tall as a zombie, as popular as a zombie, but talks a hell of a lot more."

"Oh no."

I looked up and saw my fears confirmed.

A month after my arrival at the Sheraton, I discovered four guys had mirrored my strategy a few blocks away at the Westin. As a group, they're OK. They have their strengths and weaknesses, like any collection of guys.

The one we like least is Felix. I suspect he was a smarmy misogynist before the apocalypse. He hasn't let the change in world circumstances interfere with his personality failings.

There is some tension between the groups and it is mostly his fault. Soon after meeting us, he flirted with Jess and managed to offend our entire group in the process. He explained his interest in her was due to his assessment that they were the second most attractive members of their respective groups and he didn't like his chances with the woman he liked more. I've paraphrased him slightly. His version was longer and more insulting.

In retaliation, she told him that her answer was no and would remain no if they were the last two people in the world. This is an old expression, commonly used for generations, to emphasize disinterest. However, I can assure you that the expression carries far more weight than it did in previous decades due to the statistical likelihood that the two affected parties may one day be the last two people in the world. There may even be a direct, statistical correlation between the impact of the statement and a decrease in population.

"Ladies, a pleasure as always." he said. "To what do I owe this happy coincidence?"

"We need a few supplies." Beth explained.

"A worthy quest for your intrepid team. But what brings you to the men's department."

"They're clothes. They fit me." I replied. "Are you going to tell me you have a prior claim on the stock?"

"I don't think we have anything in writing, but these are for men and I'm a man. It hardly seems fair that you can take things from here and we can't retaliate in kind."

"You have our permission to steal some dresses anytime you want." I offered.

"Thanks Essie. Maybe we'll let it go this time."

He always calls me Essie. I hate it almost as much as I hate him, although the two are intertwined in my thinking.

"On behalf of our group, I thank you for your gracious permission."

He didn't appreciate my sarcasm.

"Watch yourself." he reminded me. "It's a dangerous world out there."

"It sure is. Please go do something dangerous."

He glared at me and shook his head angrily.

"I'll never understand why you speak to me that way. You never gave me a chance."

"I had a dream in which I gave you a chance." I replied. "I woke up screaming. That's the first time that's ever happened and I live in a city overrun with the undead."

Cate, Kelly and Jess joined us before he could respond. Felix grinned for their benefit. Jess returned the least convincing smile in the history of the apocalypse.

"Ladies, I was just telling your impolite friend our news. We have a new guest."

"New?" Kelly asked excitedly. "A man or a woman?"

Cate glanced at her and Kelly tried to hide her obvious enthusiasm.

"It's another man. You're welcome to meet him. We have a party tomorrow night. I extend an official invitation."

"Thank you for the invitation." Cate replied. "Tell Marcus we accept."

Marcus was their leader. Ignoring Felix's role in the invitation and offering response to Marcus was a far more subtle slight than the one I was considering. I give Cate credit, because subtlety isn't an obvious strategy when it comes to hating Felix.

"What's he like?" Kelly asked.

In deference to Cate's wishes, she'd switched her tone to something resembling an indifferent enquiry.

"He's nothing like me." Felix replied critically.

"I like him already." I said.

He viewed our increased numbers and admitted defeat. He nodded to Cate, avoided eye contact with me, and abandoned the area.

Cate waited until he left the floor before she started to smirk. The others took this as permission to do likewise.

"What was he really telling you?" Cate asked.

"He wants us to keep out of men's clothing stores." Beth replied. "Apparently we're not men."

"I hate that guy."

"If we throw him off a roof, no one will investigate." I suggested.

Cate laughed and threw her arm around my shoulder.

"Even though I don't like him," she said. "I like you a lot more when he's around."

We finally reached the residences early afternoon, a row of townhouses with a view of the river. I can't imagine what they would have cost a buyer earlier this year. Now that the most important characteristic of a property is its height, they're worthless.

Residences typically carry the most valuable rewards, but they also carry the most danger. We have to consider the possibility that they might hold supplies we would find attractive, but we also have to consider the possibility that they might hold zombies that would find us attractive.

As we approached the first residence, Cate assigned our tasks for the duration of the mission.

"Esther, you'll be noisemaker. Kelly, Jess, you're eyes and ears. Beth is a looter. I'm emergency backup. Any questions?"

We agreed immediately. We trust Cate most of the time at the hotel, but we trust her completely when we're outdoors.

I approached the front door and scanned the view for anything closer than our scheme dictated. I took a deep breath and concentrated my stare on the front door.

"I … Am … Food!"

I waited for a response and received nothing. This didn't mean anything at only a first attempt.

"I … Am … Food!"

I heard a small noise from the nearest residence. It could have been an undead response or it could have been Beth breaking through a back window.

The noises became louder and closer. Finally, a large zombie appeared in the doorway. My every instinct told me to run. My role in the plan needed me to ignore these instincts and grant Beth more time.

"You're safe right." Kelly told me.

"You're safe left and behind." Jess confirmed.

"I could be lunch!" I yelled at the zombie. "I could be lunch!"

He took a long, awkward step forward. I was the first human he'd seen in weeks and he almost tumbled in his enthusiasm. The dried blood on his shirt told me I wouldn't be his first victim.

"It's time to run." Kelly said.

"Beth needs more time." I replied.

"Esther, get out of there."

"Beth needs more time!"

The zombie shuffled closer. I took a small step backwards as a token gesture to my terrified brain.

"Too close!" Kelly shouted. "Too close!"

Cate smashed a metal bar into the zombie's skull from behind and it collapsed at my feet.

"Too close, Esther." Cate said calmly. "Don't do that again."

I breathed a sigh of relief. Jess and Kelly couldn't decide whether to be impressed or distressed and I ignored their responses anyway. If Beth had food, it had been worth it. When Beth exited the residence, I knew from her smile that she had something good.

The legitimately paranoid resident, possibly the shuffling creature Cate had almost decapitated, had stocked his home with a collection of emergency boxes. The stash included food, medicine and other useful supplies. We were its new owners and my heroics had secured them.

It was the bravest thing I'd ever attempted. I never wanted to do it again.

The argument started ten minutes after we returned and destroyed all the goodwill our good luck had created. Kelly exploded onto our floor demanding the return of some jewellery from Gin and I jumped to Gin's defence because Gin never does.

Cate, Beth and Jess arrived within minutes. Cate and Beth attempted to calm the situation and Jess assisted her closest friend in its escalation.

In amongst the shouting, I discovered that the source of the accusation was a missing necklace. Kelly had left it in her room prior to our scavenger hunt. Gin was the only one who hadn't ventured out that day and the obvious suspect.

I didn't have evidence of Gin's innocence other than Gin's innocence. I listened to Jess and Kelly's case and my response matched their accusations in violence and volume.

The necklace wasn't the first of our items to disappear from our hotel in the past two weeks. The most common item to disappear was food, followed by basic survival gear. We'd noticed missing pieces before. We'd argued and accused each other before. Personal items were a new development and the increased emotional implications followed it into new territory.

Cate attempted to postpone the argument until she could investigate and Jess refused. In retaliation, Cate launched into an attack on Jess that concerned the question of authority more than a necklace. She shouted louder than anyone and slammed everyone that opposed her more forcefully.

"I didn't lose it. One of you stole it." Kelly repeated.

"You stole it!" I yelled, frustrated with the entire discussion. "You stole it just like you steal everything! It's lost. Steal something else."

"I didn't steal it from a store." she said quietly.

I heard her comment because our confrontation had brought us to each other's throats, but the others missed it. I placed my hand gently on Kelly's shoulder.

"I didn't take it from a store." she repeated. "I stole it from my sister, six months ago. It's all I had left of her."

Everyone saw my conciliatory gesture and realised that they'd missed an unexpected development. The shouting subsided and they watched me for my next response.

"We'll take something else." I said. "We'll take something better, something your sister would have liked."

Kelly nodded. I stepped aside and allowed Jess to take my place. The two best friends embraced and cried.

I exited the room with Gin, Cate and Beth. An inconsolable Gin disappeared to her room. I would follow her shortly and spend the next two hours rebuilding her limited confidence.

"Gin didn't steal it." I whispered to Cate.

"Someone did. Kelly's room may be a mess, but she has a system. If she says it's not there, it's not there."

"OK. Then someone took it, but it wasn't Gin."

Cate looked through the open doorway into Gin's bedroom at Kelly and Jess. She didn't explain why. If she had, she would have admitted she suspected the same person that I did.

I was told years ago that money doesn't buy happiness. I heard a supporting story that lottery wins don't change personalities. Most of the happy people who win remain happy. Most of the unhappy people stay unhappy. I don't know if it's true, but I believe it because I've seen evidence to support the theory from the opposite end of the spectrum. We survived an event of such life-changing magnitude that it should have transformed people, but it didn't. Welcome to the zombie apocalypse and the people you never liked won't have improved much.

Our world is violent. Our world is dangerous. Those of us who remained adapted quickly (we had to). Those of us who persevered reinvented our daily lives (we didn't have much of a choice). However, at heart, we're the same people we were before.

Most of the happy people who sidestepped the end of the world are still happy, all things considered. Most of the unhappy people who sidestepped the end of the world are still unhappy, although they've secured different issues on which to focus their unhappiness. The nerds and the eccentrics and the jerks are still nerds and eccentrics and jerks respectively. Our personalities are stubbornly persistent.

People always thought of me as loyal and kind. I hope that my new friends would describe me the same way. I was all those things, I'm still all of those things, and I may be an unlikely candidate for our city's few surviving humans.

Kelly, our resident fashion advisor, is a kleptomaniac, but she freely admits that she always was. The only difference is that her favourite vice became much easier. I suspect that Cate was always tough, Beth was always smart and Gin was always shy. I haven't worked out Jess yet and I never got an opportunity to work out Nora.

All of this is equally true of the boys at the Westin. Our assessment of them would probably be better if they had let the circumstances influence them more than it has.

Every time the boys host a party, they schedule it for early evening because they want us to delay past dusk and sleep at their hotel instead of walking home in the dark. In retaliation, we arrive early afternoon and leave during daylight.

We've established an unofficial routine for this. They feign surprise at our early arrival. We apologize for the misunderstanding and everyone laughs. They hide their disappointment and then they forgive us because we're the only six women they know.

Cate has explained her philosophy on this several times, and several times more to Kelly. If Cate ever stays over, it will be because she decided to stay over, not because the boys tricked her into it. Kelly has argued the benefits of pretending to fall for it, perhaps once. It's a line of thinking that angers Cate.

Cate believes that if we lose the boy's respect, we'll never regain it. She wants us to prove that we are better than they are, without exception. She's never explained why this is so important to her, but we rarely question her logic because she's better than us, every day, in almost every way. We're alive because of Cate and we never forget it.

Cate called a meeting before the party, a predictable step that preceded every excursion outside of our home. She came to visit the eighth floor before the meeting, an unexpected courtesy that caught me off guard. I jumped to a conclusion, albeit a wrong one, and predicted my selection as the hotel's guardian for the evening and the sole absentee from the party.

"I should stay." I said. "It's my turn."

Whoever she selected would be unhappy. She has a tough job leading us and I wanted to make her decision easier.

"No." Cate replied. "You should go. You should meet the new guy. I hear he's perfect for you."

"We know nothing about him."

"We know he's not like Felix and that's a good start. … Go. Have fun. You earned it when you played bait for those supplies. We should make that a rule. Anyone who plays bait deserves a party."

"Is that the only reason?" I asked suspiciously.

"No, I want Jess to take a turn."

"You think something will go missing again?"

"No. If you're right and she thinks we're stupid, nothing will."

"I never said I suspected Jess."

"You didn't, but you didn't need to. I suspect her and you're smarter than me."

Marcus is the bravest member of The Westin group, but not necessarily the most intelligent. He is happy, friendly and semi-permanently drunk in order to perpetuate his non-negotiable happiness. Marcus is their leader by default because of the quality of the other candidates.

Aiden is the survivor of an ordeal he hasn't confessed in detail to anyone and possibly crazy as a result of the trauma. Ilya is handsome, foreign and speaks no English. The fourth member of the group is Felix, a man as devoted to being unlikeable as Marcus is to inebriation.

Han was the newest member of this diverse, dysfunctional group.

I liked him the first time I saw him. Maybe that is circumstance. Maybe that was a response to the recent stresses we'd all suffered. Maybe it was the possibility that there were only five men left alive and I didn't particularly like the other four. Whatever the reason, I liked him immediately.

I was conflicted. Part of me wanted to meet a new human being in a city that didn't boast many. Another part of me wanted to meet a new survivor who could have prolonged his survival by acquiring items from a nearby Sheraton without permission.

He was a suspect. They all were. I knew I liked him because of how much I wanted to exclude him from my informal investigation and obtain evidence against one of the others.

I got an opportunity to speak to him soon after my arrival. Cate, a blunt and clumsy matchmaker, demanded his attention, demanded mine, and then abandoned us. I've never liked her more.

I told him my name was Esther. We talked around a number of subjects, including his survival and self-imposed exile at the Hyatt. He'd recently fled from some zombie stalkers who'd determined his hiding place after several weeks and a noisy process of elimination.

Our conversation lasted for more than an hour in which we anti-socially shunned everyone else. I was happy to continue both the conversation and the shunning.

We eventually returned to the subject of his unusual name.

"So, Han, like the Solo?"

"Actually, it's short for Hannibal like the Lecter."

"Did your parents name you after the General?" I asked.

"No, they pretty much named me after the Lecter."

"Wow, that's rough. ... Although it is kind of ironic that you're one of the few creatures left in the city who isn't trying to eat human body parts."

"Under different circumstances, I might consider it a last laugh, if there were fewer zombies, and more laughing."

I realized how insensitive my comment was and apologized. I hoped he understood.

"I'm sorry." I said. "We've been through a lot. We've developed a strange sense of humour."

"It's fine. It's a good line. It's just ... Did you ever see I Am Legend with Will Smith. You know the way he goes a little crazy because it's been years and he only has a dog for company? Then, he meets someone, but he's forgotten how to talk to another person. I know how that feels, only I got there faster because I don't have a dog."

"You thought you were alone on Monday. Today, you're at a party thrown in your honour. It's a lot to process."

He smiled at me in way that should have captured my heart, but only broke it a little.

"Thank you." he said.

"What did I do?"

"You're still alive. It's the nicest thing anyone could have done for me."

I didn't want to spoil the moment. It was my favourite evening for a very long time. As a compromise, I allowed my internal detective to sneak a single question into the conversation. I didn't realize that Felix had appeared behind me.

"This may sound like a crazy question, but in all that time you were out there, did you ever go into the Sheraton?"

"Some of their things went for a walk." Felix said. "She wants to know if you took them. That's why she wanted to talk to you so much."

I tried to defend myself, but my excuses fell flat as I tried to determine the accuracy of the unflattering claim.

I could tell that Han was upset. He'd liked me as much as I'd liked him and it appeared misleadingly as if I'd needed a hidden agenda to speak with him.

"I see. … No, I never stole anything from the Sheraton because I spent the last few days fighting my way north and trying *really hard* not to die. The closest I ever got to the river was … here. It was here. The closest I ever got to the river was here. And I've never set foot in the Sheraton."

"I'm sorry. … I didn't …"

"That's OK. That's the world we live in. You had to rule me out of your enquiries and I'm glad I'm no longer a suspect."

He walked away and hovered by the side of another group. He listened in to the increasingly drunken ramblings of Kelly. Ilya hung on Kelly's every word without actually understanding any of her words.

"Oops. Did I say the wrong thing?" Felix asked.

"What do you know about things that went for a walk?"

"I know everything about them. Kelly hasn't shut up about her necklace since she arrived. Why? Do you want to blame me next?"

"I would like to because it would give me another reason to hate you. Never mind; I just remembered that I don't need another reason. Good-bye."

"You're leaving so soon?"

"Some parties have it. Some parties don't have it. And this one? This one's got you."

I walked over towards my friends.

"I'm heading back. Anyone want to join me?"

"I want to stay." Kelly announced.

Ilya appeared to like her decision, despite not knowing what she'd decided.

Gin agreed to join me because she suspected she would retreat further into her shell if I departed. Beth and Cate debated the benefits of staying for another 30 minutes, but reconsidered. They joined us for reasons they didn't share, but that I guessed anyway. Cate wanted to know if anything was missing, and she wanted to know before Gin arrived back at the Sheraton.

Beth took the lead on our way back, a crucial responsibility that we instinctively rotated through the group. Cate drifted to the back and I slowed my pace until I was alongside her.

There was something I wanted to ask her, perhaps motivated by the conclusion to my evening.

We have a running joke. Every day, one of us asks Cate why we don't live with the boys. In response, Cate improvises a different answer each time. The first time someone asked her she replied that the boys would get us killed. The second time she claimed that they smell bad. She's flirted with a wide variety of explanations since.

For some reason, I wanted to be the one to ask her today. For the first time since we'd started the tradition, she answered honestly instead of joking.

"Do you think I run things better than Marcus?"

"Yes." I told her.

It was true. It wasn't even close.

"So does he. That's why we don't live with the boys. ... Why do you ask?"

I considered lying. I wasn't sure I wanted to admit how much I cared about Han's opinion.

"I think I made a bad first impression."

"He'll forgive you. You're smart *and* pretty. There's not many left like you."

"What about you?"

"What about me?'

"You're incredible. You're the most amazing person I know."

"Ha. Those guys are scared of me because I'm tougher than they are. They don't know how to deal with it. We live in a messed-up world where the ability to break some bones is more valuable than ever, but none of them would chase after a girl who could kick his ass. Bunch of morons don't deserve me. I'll think I'll concentrate on keeping you idiots alive instead."

"On behalf of our idiots, thank you."

"Zombie." Beth said.

We made our instinctive step to the side and continued our journey.

"I still like guys," Cate muttered. "... but seriously, have you seen what's available?"

We re-joined the others as we entered through the lobby, often the most dangerous part of any journey outside. We climbed the stairs without incident and tried our best to ignore the moans of the zombie on 5.

He (I've always assumed it's a he) has lived here longer than we have. I've never seen him. He gives us our space due to an effective barricade that he apparently can't defeat. We give him his space out of respect for his probable eating habits.

His other contribution, other than our caution near his habitat, is the inspiration behind our most frequent insult. It's one that appears, sometimes more than once, in most of our arguments. Anytime someone says something we don't like, we tell them to try living on 5. I've told Jess to move to 5 a few times. She's suggested the same to me.

When we arrived on 8, the floor I shared with Gin, I invited her to sleep in the spare bed of my double room. I appreciated the company. I wanted Gin to have an alibi.

Light sleep is easy to accomplish for a variety of reasons that include exhaustion and malnutrition. Heavy sleep is more difficult to obtain. For this reason, I wake very quickly if two people start a shouting match two floors above me.

I recognised the owners of the voices as Cate and Jess before I opened my eyes. I guessed the reason for the argument before I sat up. Someone had stolen one of the emergency supply boxes we'd recovered from the house by the river.

Gin and I were the last to arrive. Beth stood silently on the side-lines as the disagreement escalated. I didn't know who was right, but I was certain Cate would win. I was surprised Jess didn't know this. If she did, she didn't care.

I listened to their accusations and counter accusations. Cate threw insults of selfishness and betrayal at Jess. Jess retaliated with accusations of her own, claims that had no basis other than the need to blame Cate as loudly as Cate blamed her. Both women predictably suggested a move to 5 and the probable demise that involved.

I tried to ignore the raised voices and thought through the possibilities. It was another crime. It was another robbery by someone who had no alibi for any of the instances. It was another theft from an unprotected floor, under the nose of a guardian left to protect our possessions, by someone familiar with what we possessed.

"It wasn't Jess." I said.

The fight missed my statement and continued regardless.

"She didn't take our things." I said again. "And I know who did."

The argument stopped abruptly.

I paused for as long as I thought they would accept.

"When was the last time anyone saw the zombie on 5?"

Gin, Beth and Jess exited the hotel and walked towards the Westin. Jess wore her favourite designer jacket, Beth wore her hair down and Gin was shorter than both of them by 12 inches. From a distance, they were easy to identify.

Cate and I waited patiently and silently on nine, in the corridor outside Kelly's room. Cate wasn't convinced by my theory, but she was curious enough to test it.

Five minutes after their departure, we heard noises from inside the elevator shaft. We waited silently until someone forced the doors open and climbed onto nine, the only one of our floors that was supposed to be empty.

She was slightly shorter than me, slightly plainer, slightly more athletic. She wore her hair in a practical, convenient pony-tail and her dirty clothes suggested she hadn't raided as many stores as we had. She looked the same as the last time I had seen her.

Our thief was Nora.

She allowed the doors to close quietly. We remained quiet and she didn't see us until she turned towards Kelly's room. She collapsed backwards and slammed loudly into the metal of the elevator.

"We thought you were dead." Cate said dispassionately. "We were sad about that."

Nora looked at me for confirmation.

"We really were." I added, with a little more sincerity and emotion.

Nora pulled herself into a sitting position.

"Can you blame me?" she said. "Look at the world we're in. I don't know if anything is wrong anymore."

"We can agree to disagree." Cate replied.

Cate was yet to raise her voice, but if this discussion turned violent, Nora was in trouble.

"Is there still a zombie on five?" I asked.

"He's there, but I blocked him in. He's loud, but I'd rather deal with one zombie than a hundred. I'm not going out there again."

"Yes, you are." Cate said.

She explained it in the same confident, uncaring tone in which she'd said everything else. We hadn't discussed possible punishments before Nora's arrival because Cate had dismissed its possibility. I realised that she'd since determined the verdict and the punishment.

"Do the others know?" Nora asked.

"They will soon. They walked around the block and they should be on five by now. We'll be taking back all the things you stole."

"How did you work it out? Was it the necklace?"

"Does it matter?" Cate told her.

For some reason, despite my contribution to events, I sympathised more with the culprit than I'd thought I would. Part of me was disappointed by what she'd done. The rest of me was happy she was alive.

"Yes, it was the necklace." I said.

Nora stood up and looked at the closed elevator doors. With the need for secrecy gone, she'd lost her enthusiasm for the extra effort it required.

"Can I take the staircase?"

Cate nodded and Nora walked towards the corridor's exit. Cate followed after her for every flight of stairs and watched her evade zombies for two blocks.

I didn't ask Cate what she would have done if Nora had refused to leave. Nora didn't ask either, but I think we guessed the same.

"We have a problem?" Beth said.

Jess and Gin appeared behind her, exhausted after their sprint up the stairs.

"What kind of …" Cate started to say. "How many?"

"I don't know. Maybe four or five hundred. It's enough that my guess could be short and I wouldn't know."

"Does that qualify as a horde?" I asked.

"Half a thousand zombies?" Cate replied. "They can call themselves anything they want and I'll play along. Where are they?"

"It's the Westin." Beth said. "It's surrounded. They used the corridors."

The corridors are a network of pathways that connect the second floor of all downtown's towers. Back when the city was a bustling commercial centre, the corridors had enabled everyone to travel from one end of the city's core to the other without straying outside if the temperatures dropped. We'd avoided the corridors in recent weeks because the wideness of the streets made for safer journeys than the narrow hallways.

"I told them they needed to watch the corridors." Cate said. "Do you know what they said?"

"I believe it was 'We've got that covered, thank you.'" Beth replied.

Cate turned to look at me and provided today's punch line for the running joke.

"And that is why we don't live with the boys."

We gathered in the communal area on 10 to discuss our next move. Jess had fallen silent after learning the scale of the danger and registering that Kelly was in the middle of it. Gin hadn't contributed to the discussion, but she rarely did. We needed a solution and it looked like it needed to come from Beth, Cate or me. I had nothing realistic or unexpected.

"Use me." I said. "Use me as bait. I'll make a fuss. They'll chase me. You get them out."

"It's too risky." Cate replied.

"I have to try. It's me for six people."

"It won't work." Beth explained. "We need the attention of the horde's centre. The back of the horde could tear you apart before the centre knows you're there."

The room fell into silence. With no new ideas of my own, I tried to provoke and inspire the suggestions of others.

"We can't get as close as we need to. How else do we get their attention?"

I looked at Beth, who looked at Cate, who looked at me. None of us looked at Gin.

"Could we blow something up?" Gin asked.

Cate's sat up straight and her eyes widened. She immediately gave us roles, much as she would for a routine scavenger hunt.

"Gin, you're our eyes and ears from the base of the Sheraton. You need to warn us if we lose our retreat. Beth, you're our backup. Jess, I need you to get to a neighbouring building, get the boys a message."

"What's the message?" Jess asked, eager to be part of the rescue mission.

"We're going to set their home on fire. But it's not personal. We're setting fire to a lot of things."

Cate, Beth and I paused one block from the horde and reviewed our plan.

"We have to move fast." Cate said. "They'll get outside the store and block our retreat."

"What are you thinking?" I asked.

"Molotov cocktail."

"You mean like a liquor bottle?"

"No, I mean like a liquor store."

She passed me one of the two metal pipes she'd brought with her. It was heavier than I'd imagined. I'd underestimated the muscles she'd developed from swinging it on a daily basis.

"Are you ready to make some noise?" she said.

"Let's save some lives." I replied.

We ran around the corner and sprinted at the largest gathering of monsters I'd ever seen. I screamed with every step. I aimed for where the density was lightest, close enough to touch them and fast enough that they couldn't touch me. Cate followed behind me, swinging at anything that glanced my way. I continued my irregular path, calling for their attention and listening to Cate punish anyone who responded.

We reached the liquor store and I jumped through a missing pane in the large front window. Cate followed. We took a moment and I caught my breath.

"You ready?" she asked.

I didn't know. I nodded anyway.

"Start smashing." she instructed.

I started with the vodkas. Cate selected the most expensive bottle behind the counter, cracked its lid and stuffed a rag in the top. I worked my way along the side wall and swung at everything in sight. Within seconds, I was soaked and standing in a small lake of alcohol.

I turned as I heard a groan. A giant zombie blocked the empty window pane.

"Visitors." I shouted.

"Clear a path."

I picked up a bottle of wine and threw a perfect fastball into the zombie's face. Then I swung the pipe into a neighbouring window pane and created a new exit. I saw more zombies drifting in our direction.

"We've got to go." I shouted.

"Then go!"

I launched trough the new gap and struck out at everyone within reach. I caught one creature below his chin and he catapulted backwards into more of his group. I saw Cate leap towards me and we started our sprint to safety.

She threw a lit cocktail behind her and it arced through the air towards the store. I watched it fall and stumbled as my twisted body watched its flight. Cate grabbed me without slowing her pace and dragged me on.

As we broke clear of the horde, a rain of tiny missiles fell from the sky, a well-timed distraction from Jess to aid our retreat. As we turned the corner, Beth met us. I threw the metal bar to her and she caught it with perfect reflexes. She and Cate held their bats ready for anything that tried to follow, but nothing did.

"Did it work?" I asked from my position on the floor.

"It'll work," Cate replied. "or fail really loudly."

The store exploded a second later. The fireball obliterated everything it touched. It turned the heads of everything within five blocks, including those already in the Westin. The flames passed from zombie to zombie and spread throughout the crowd.

I picked myself up, more calm than I should have been, energised by the success of the plan.

"We can go." I said. "The boys know where to find us."

We watched from Gin's room as a window smashed on the Westin's fourth floor and someone threw a mattress onto the one storey extension below. Five more mattresses followed. Predictably, Marcus was the first to attempt the jump.

He landed expertly on the makeshift safety net and prepared for the next arrival. Han leapt next. Kelly followed third and they caught her as she landed. One by one, they fled their burning home as smoke escaped from each of the hotel's broken windows. Felix jumped last. Cate looked at me as he landed, safe and uninjured.

"No plan is perfect." I suggested.

Cate smiled and punched my shoulder. She likes me more when Felix is around.

"We owe you." Marcus told Cate.

"Oh, I know."

"Name it and it's yours."

"Don't rush us. We'll want to give this some thought."

The last survivor to arrive on the Sheraton's tenth floor was Felix. His unpleasant personality, already a survivor of the end of the world, remained equally unimpressed by our rescue.

"We would have made it out without you." he announced to the room.

He stared critically at me as he said it. Given a few more moments, I'm confident I would have devised a killer response. He brings that out in me. I didn't get the opportunity.

"Shut up, Felix." Marcus said loudly.

He'd previously allowed Felix's comments to go uncorrected, but we were untouchable today. Apparently Felix hadn't received that memo.

"I'm sorry about Felix." Marcus said. "He has his own unique language and that's how you say thank you in moron. That's going to change. We'll teach him to use different words from now on. It's the least we can do."

"Thank you." I said. "We'd appreciate that."

The two groups mingled and regaled each other with different parts of the tale, most of which we knew but all of which were a joy to hear again.

I sought out Han, hoping that his goodwill might extend to accepting my apology. I pulled him to one side and he followed me happily.

"I never thought you stole our things." I told him.

"None of that matters now." he replied. "I saw what you did."

"You saw it?" I asked, a little embarrassed.

"I had a perfect view from executive box seats. I know one of your friends was in our building, but if you want to claim that you ran through a horde of zombies to save me, I'll believe you. I'm in your debt forever."

"I think I can handle eternal gratitude."

"It's yours."

Marcus called everyone to the centre of the room. I thought it was presumptuous of him to take control of the gathering, but Cate said nothing and so I didn't either.

"We need a plan." Marcus said. "We can't stay here."

"You're welcome." Jess interrupted. "You can go back to your hotel anytime you want. The flames may be out by now."

"Marcus is right." Beth said. "The explosion attracted their attention and set up the escape, but everything for miles heard it and they're shuffling this way as we speak. … We need to move."

If Beth thought we were in danger, we all believed her, but deciding to leave and deciding where to go were two very different questions. Everyone looked to everyone else for suggestions.

"… We go to the Hyatt." Han said.

"You left the Hyatt a week ago." I reminded him.

"Exactly, and I left it because it was surrounded by zombies. I left and they've stalked me ever since. However, if Beth is right, they heard the blast and they'll walk this way. All we have to do is loop around the side of them. It will take them weeks to know we've fooled them and several more weeks to walk back the way they came. If we set it up right, we could just switch between the two hotels a couple of times a year."

"So, less of a fight for our lives and more of a timeshare arrangement?"

"… OK, that's not exactly what I was thinking, but I see the analogy."

"Don't apologise. I love the idea."

We looked to the rest of the room. They all approved, except for Felix who was predisposed to disapproving of everything for the rest of the day.

I looked at Beth, hoping she could help me with the calculations.

"But we don't need to go right now, right?"

"A couple of blocks, standard rate of progress, allowance for the distraction of an unexpected inferno. We'll be swarmed and surrounded if we're still here on Saturday."

"So, we flee for our lives … Thursday?" I suggested.

Cate and Beth smiled. Marcus agreed. Receiving their endorsement secured the support of everyone else. The overall strategy confirmed, we started to refine details. By the time we'd finished, our plan was perfect.

That's the world we live in. Even when we face incredible odds, we face them on a relaxed schedule. We're the calm in the storm. We're the centre of the hurricane. We may be the children of the apocalypse, but we've decided to deal with it later.

A Short Conversation

A very short story.

"I'm writing another novel." I said.

"That's great news."

"It's going to be shorter than the last one."

"That's even better news."

We both laughed because he's a good friend and it's a longstanding, private joke.

"And it's going to be a comedy." I added.

"That's … Sorry. What did you say?"

"It's a comedy. I'm trying to write something funny."

From a certain perspective, the silence that followed was an interesting, eloquent response.

"Are you sure?" he asked eventually.

"That's what I'm trying. Why?"

"You've looked kind of serious lately."

"I always look serious. That's just my face."

"No. I mean, yes, you always look serious, but what I mean is, recently you've looked, you know, serious."

"Oh. OK. Good to know."

"But you're serious about being, you know, funny."

"That's the plan."

"Does that mean you're going to smile more?"

"Oh no, that's just crazy talk."

A Whole Other Sinister Level

A very short story.

Jay balanced himself on the top of the crumbling, stone arch. He stared into the distance with such intensity and focus that he didn't hear George approaching.

George tried to follow his friend's line of sight from the haunted graveyard to the dying forest, but saw only trees of various heights, shades and ages. He watched as Jay carefully repeated the same phrases and expressions over and over. At first, it looked ominous, but it quickly evolved into something more predictable.

"If you're hoping that looks spooky," he said. "I have to warn you, it's starting to look neurotic."

Jay snapped out of his concentration.

"I have some things I am trying to memorize."

"OK. … Because?"

"… I don't want to tell you." Jay replied cautiously.

"Why don't you want to tell me?"

"I don't want to tell you that either."

"OK. … Because?"

"You'll laugh."

"Now I really want you to tell me."

"Do you promise not to laugh?"

"If you promise this is something that might make me laugh, I believe you. If I then promise that you can trust me not to laugh, you can't believe me."

Jay's instinct told him that nothing good would come from honesty. His instinct also told him that nothing good would come from keeping the secret.

"It's homework."

George pulled a strange, contorted expression that appeared even stranger on his ghostly face.

"What are you doing?" Jay said.

"You asked me not to laugh. This is my not-laughing face. If you'll excuse me for a moment, this expression will require my concentration and willpower for another minute."

George held the expression. Jay waited for it to fade before he re-joined the conversation.

"I had to do something. I've run the same act for months and it isn't working. I need to shake it up, take it to a whole other sinister level, and be all that I can be. This is the something I selected. The course is called Paranormal Basics and Alternate Haunting Techniques."

George kept a straight face for a few short seconds and then disappeared into hysterics. Each time Jay tried to interrupt the laughter, Jay held up a hand to indicate that he needed another few moments.

"You want to be all that you can be?" George said finally. "Did you really say that out loud? Do you want me to do the face again?"

"I knew it was a mistake to tell you."

"And that's really your motive?"

"It's an interesting course. There's a lot of useful knowledge, some transferable skills and some insight into the challenges we face. The instructor is excellent. The group are a fascinating mix of motives and interests and experience. I honestly believe any open-minded spectre would benefit from the content."

"OK. Yes. You make some good points." George said.

He drifted onto the arch next to his friend and stared into the darkness. Jay resumed with the justification for his return to school.

"Next week, we look at a new approach to telekinesis and you know I've always struggled with the poltergeist routine. This is what I need. This is what I have to do if I want to raise my game."

"I'm sorry and you're right. I should have reserved judgment until I had given you a chance to describe it. It sounds worthwhile." George conceded.

He paused for effect and then asked his next question.

"... What's her name?"

Jay turned to look at George and stumbled over his reply.

"... Who?"

"Whoever it is that's in the class that inspired you to take the class."

"I didn't convince you with the 'be all I can be'?"

"Jay, you're dead. All you can be is varying degrees of translucent."

George hadn't bought it for a moment. The quality of Jay's misleading explanation was undermined completely by the predictability of Jay's personality.

"… I am enjoying the course." Jay said.

"And I'm sure you love homework too. Who is she?"

"… Her name is Gemma. She's relatively new to our world. She's very sweet. I think she'll struggle for a while. I'm not sure she has the heart for it."

"She sounds lovely. Are you going to mess it up?"

Jay's expression twisted into a combination of disappointment and outrage.

"You're my friend and you know me better than anybody. What kind of a question is that?"

"You're right. I'm sorry. So, how do you *think* you'll mess it up?"

Jay hesitated and his outrage faded.

"Yeah, I did give that some thought, based on prior, embarrassing history. I think there are three leading candidates. Number one: I never actually confess to her that I like her."

"Possible. There's precedent."

"There *is* precedent."

"There's *a lot of precedent*. What's number 2?"

"She's not looking for a relationship right now."

"Plausible. New ghost. Uncertain future. I can see that. Number 3?"

"She's open to a relationship right now, but not with me."

"Very plausible."

"Can something be very plausible? Surely it is or it isn't."

"What's a better word for more than plausible?"

"I don't know. Likely?"

"Then it's likely, and I strongly suggest you criticize her word selection if you need a fourth leading candidate to add to the other three."

George read his friend's expression and considered the likelihood that all the misfortune they were predicting was the most probable turn of events.

"You really like her, don't you?"

Jay nodded.

"How serious is this?" George said.

"It's serious enough to take a course with homework."

"Ha. I knew it. I knew you weren't enjoying the homework. … But I will leave you to it."

"Thank you."

George floated to the far side of the graveyard, the corner of their domain in which he was least likely to disrupt Jay's work. Jay returned to his memory phrases and fact recitation.

It still wasn't frightening.

It still looked kind of neurotic.

The British are Visiting

A short story.

Robert arrived five minutes early. The man at the entrance greeted him with an unimpressed scowl.

"I am here to see Nat Glinn." Robert explained.

A smartly dressed and unimpressed staff member confirmed Robert's identity and then permitted him inside the exclusive restaurant.

"I will take you to your table." he said in a way that suggested the short journey would be an inconvenience and the lowest point of his day.

Robert followed him through the establishment. He passed four Hollywood producers and seven actors of varying notoriety. Some of them glanced up, but none of them recognised him. Despite Robert's success in Britain, this was new. This was a whole other world.

Robert was an Englishman of eastern European descent. He possessed a serious face and a reluctant smile. He looked like a Shakespearean villain who would be permitted to talk to the audience.

The seating arrangements in the restaurant appeared to revolve around fame, with the popular and the notorious within view of the entrance and the locally anonymous hidden on the far side. Robert received a table against the back wall.

Five minutes after his arrival, Robert accepted a small, expensive bottle of water he hadn't ordered. He sat quietly and scanned the area for more faces he could identify. He saw a news correspondent, a talk show host and a politician. He saw two people he assumed to be writers, taking notes from a studio executive's monologue. It made for strangely compelling entertainment.

He waited five additional minutes before realizing that Nat, his new American agent, was eating at the table around the corner from his obscured view. Nat greeted him like an old friend and excused himself from his meal and previous conversation.

"I love this place." Nat explained. "I eat here every day if I can, and I can. It's difficult to get a table, but I have three because I eat here every day and I tell everyone who is anyone to eat here every day. You see the executive over there, the one making the writers cry? I told him about this place. He tried it because of me. Now he's here once a week making writers cry. Have you ordered? I ordered. Everything is good. The server will frown like you ordered wrong, but you can't order wrong because everything is right. I won't order, I have food at the other table, but you should order. It's on me. I eat here all the time and it's good."

Nat talked faster than anyone Robert had ever met. Robert squeezed in a brief thank you before Nat set off again.

"There's someone I want you to meet today. You'll like him. He talks your language. He knows your story. He's *lived* your story. I think the two of you will be great friends until you're not. He should be here any moment. Order something. I'll be back in five minutes."

Nat stood up. Instead of returning to his meal, he weaved his way to a third setting, greeting everyone on the way, all of whom he seemed to know. The only person he didn't disturb was the executive who was mid-thought and mid-sentence.

Nat sat at a table with a young, good-looking man. Robert guessed at a potential client, perhaps a model interested in a transition to acting. The theory explained the man's looks and Nat's presence.

A server approached and offered to take Robert's order. Robert selected the cheapest item on the expensive menu. The waiter hesitated and frowned, as if Robert had answered incorrectly.

Robert's attention shifted to a new arrival, an English comic that Robert recognized from British television. The comedian crossed the floor quickly, evading the staff and ignoring their questions. He slipped easily past the famous and not-so-famous diners without distracting them. He'd won awards in Britain, but he was as anonymous in this restaurant as Robert.

Unlike Robert, the comic was a northerner. Unlike Robert, he'd come from a background with no money and few prospects. Robert knew all of this because the comic's early struggles were a key part of his routine, a vicious, hilarious commentary on British geography and customs.

The man walking towards him differed from the onscreen comic, but he was almost at the table by the time Robert identified it. There was something jaded about his movement and expression. The confident swagger Robert would have predicted was missing. Maybe the town had beaten him. Maybe he was always this way off stage.

The comic reached Robert's table.

"Hi, I'm Alan Mark."

Robert stood, they shook hands and then both men sat down.

"I know who you are." Robert said. "I'm a fan."

"Thank you. The feeling's mutual. I saw you in The West End about two years ago. And call me Mark. All my friends call me Mark and I think we'll be friends until we're not."

Before Robert could ask about the expression, Nat returned to the table.

"Mark, great to see you. I heard about the thing. We should talk later."

"They hated me." Mark explained.

"They didn't hate you. They don't hate anybody. They went in a different direction."

"Yeah, a direction they didn't hate."

"Mark, they didn't hate you. They loved you. Everyone loves you. They tried something else and we should talk later, but we should talk about Robert first because he's here, he hasn't eaten, and he doesn't want to talk about the thing. Robert, did you order?"

"Yes."

"Did the server say you ordered wrong or did he do the frown? He frowned, didn't he? That's because you're new. They criticize me. I love it when they criticize the order. I eat here every day. Where was I? Mark, I invited you because Robert is filled with excitement and enthusiasm and everything you've lost since you lost the thing. Robert, I invited you because you're new in town, you don't know anyone and you could use some friends until you make friends, and no one has told you the rule."

He didn't explain what he was talking about, but Mark nodded as if he understood perfectly.

"Did you fly him out or did they invite him?" Mark asked.

"I invited him and I flew him out. I want him to meet and greet." Nat replied. "It's going to be awkward if nobody tells him the rule. I think it would be better from you because you get it. I know it, but you get it. Can you tell it?"

"... Yeah, I can tell it."

"And order something. It's all good."

Nat paused briefly at his first table and then returned to his third.

"You're not saying much." Mark said.

"I was waiting for a pause in the conversation." Robert replied.

"You'll be waiting a long time. ... I hate this place."

"The town or the restaurant?"

"The restaurant. I love the town. It's a great town. I hate the restaurant and half the people in the town. I hate Nat too. I may have to fire him or kill him. I haven't decided which, but I'll have to pick one soon because he's going to drop me as a client."

The server approached Mark.

"Oh. It's you." the server said dismissively.

"Yeah, I'm ecstatic to be here too. Bring me four bottles of beer, each different, no American, four different glasses, each chilled, with a style of glass to suit each beer, and no American. Yes, I said it twice. If I don't like the beers you select or the glasses, I'll send it all back and keep sending it back until you get it right. Have a nice day."

The server skulked away and Mark explained his survival philosophy.

"Nat thinks they're fun. I think they're unprofessional. So, when they're unprofessional, I have some fun. They *do not like it*. You're supposed to behave a certain way in this town and I've stopped behaving. I didn't work this hard and achieve this much to smile politely at really bad service. And not just bad service, but conscious, pro-actively coordinated bad service. I don't belong here. It's that simple. It's possible you don't either, but that's for you to figure out."

Robert sipped at his water. It tasted like water.

"And that brings us to the rule." Mark continued. "Nat's right. It might be the last time Nat is right about anything he ever tells you, but he's right about this. If you're going to work here, you need to know the rule. And the rule is this ... Never Forget You Are English."

"That's it?"

"That's mostly it. There's subtext. And the subtext applies to a comic from a rainy, northern city they've never heard of as much as it does to a classically trained theatre actor they don't sufficiently respect and every Englishman in between."

The server brought Robert's food and Mark's drinks. Mark grinned at the bottles, contemplated how much trouble he wanted to cause, and then kept it simple for the benefit of his guest.

"Excellent choices. Thank you very much."

He waited for the server's departure before admitting his dilemma.

"My personal record is four. I wanted to send it back a fifth time, but I was laughing too much. I couldn't bring myself to do it. It's like that Marx Brothers scene, you know?"

"Too many people in the room."

"Exactly. Too many people in the room. It's funny until it's not. You've got to know when to cut. The day Nat brings me here to drop me as a client, I'm going for seven. I'll play it like a farewell tour."

Mark selected one of the four drinks. He poured into the nearest chilled glass and took a long swig.

"How does my being English play into meet and greets?" Robert asked.

"That, my friend, is the subtext." Mark replied. "If you are English and male, you are permitted to appear in American movies, but only within clearly defined roles. It is my privilege and honour to explain the guidelines by which you are hereby expected to abide."

Robert took the first bite of his salad and awaited his instructions. The salad tasted like salad.

"All Englishmen," Mark began, "regardless of height, weight, appearance and age can be the villain. You can be the villain even if the film is set outside of England as your villainy is not geographically constrained. You are permitted to be more interesting and memorable than the hero, but only within the context of committing acts that encourage the audience to hate you and wish your downfall. This downfall should be appropriate to the genre. Examples include romantic rejection, comical humiliation and animated defeat at the hands of talking animals. Your downfall will be death in almost every other film type, or death, implausible recovery and death again if its horror."

"OK."

"If you are looking for something a little heavier, you are permitted to be the central character in a character study if the character the character study studies has a flawed character. This is allowed because a study of the flaws of an imperfect, non-American character implies that Americans may indeed be perfect."

"Am I ever permitted to be the hero?"

"Yes, as an Englishmen, you are permitted to be the hero, but only within one of the following non-negotiable situations.

"If the character is a famous person from history whose English nationality is a well-known piece of public knowledge, then the character is allowed to remain English. However, the movie studio will seriously consider casting an American in the role. They will have a line of thinking that says something like 'If the historical figure was that special, they'd probably have more in common with modern-day Americans anyway'. Also, please note that important, historical figures are not the same as famous, historical figures. If they did something remarkable, but most people don't know their name, they can be rewritten as American.

"If the character is a famous literary character whose nationality is well known, again, their nationality can remain intact. However, casting an American in the role is again an option. Please note that well known, literary figures are not the same as celebrated or award winning characters. If the book won awards, but no one read it, the character can be American. And if the character is well-known and English, but the author is dead, there might be a workaround there too.

"Finally, you may be permitted to play the hero if you are indisputably good looking. Ten years ago, they referred to this as the Orlando Bloom Exception. However, if the studio includes an English actor in a central, heroic role, they will balance it with the inclusion of several, villainous

Englishmen in the same movie. Ideally the ratio of evil Englishmen to heroic Englishmen should be three to one or greater. I mention this for full disclosure, but I don't think either one of us is Orlando Bloom.

"These examples aside, wherever possible, the hero should be American, or a Canadian who passes for American and rarely advertises his country of birth. Oh, they might make an exception for an Australian if enough American women want to sleep with him."

"Are there any other available roles?"

"A story can include an Englishmen as a mentor who helps, advises or inspires the hero. The movie can emphasize the character's wisdom and education without implying that he is in any way heroic or cool. The story should also imply he has a serious character flaw, or perhaps several, to compensate for the admission that he might be intelligent. And depending on the genre, the mentor may be required to go crazy, die or both."

"Next you're going to tell me I never get the girl."

"You're getting the hang of this. As an Englishman, you never get the girl. However, if the movie features a love triangle, you are permitted to appear as the guy who *doesn't* get the girl. This character should also be used as a comparative individual whose relative weaknesses exaggerate the strengths of the hero. The story should portray an obvious decision for the leading lady. If there is any ambiguity about which man she should choose, to the point where audience opinion may be split, both men should be American."

Mark downed the rest of his first beer and carefully selected his second drink from the remaining three.

"The next is my lifeline. You may appear in a smaller, comical role. The story may portray your character as weak, uncool, old-fashioned or dull in some regard. Depending on the director or the studio, it might be a clumsy allegory that somehow implies all Englishmen are weak, uncool, old-fashioned or dull because they believe insulting an entire non-American nation is funnier than insulting one fictional person. Do you want to take another guess?"

"... Cowards?"

"Yes, definitely. You're a natural at this. Englishmen are always allowed to portray cowards or initially brave souls who later turn into cowards. This can be used as a means of demonstrating the seriousness and danger of a situation without compromising the bravery of any American characters."

"Is that all?"

"No, there is one final category. The studio might include an Englishman in a story if they wish to introduce diversity into an otherwise less-than-diverse group of characters. However, the conclusion of the Englishman's personal story must be unhappier than the conclusion of the hero's. Americans watch films for different reasons, but few of them watch movies to see an English guy win. More animals make it out of disaster movies than Englishmen for a reason.

"I've explained all this for your benefit, but these guidelines also apply to non-American, non-English actors pretending to be English, even if they can do the accent."

Robert's eyes drifted around the room while he digested the information. Mark's eyes focused on the table and he drank some more beer.

"Nat flew me in for five meetings." Robert said. "What do you think I should do?"

Mark smiled.

"Treat it like a part and play it. You're an actor, aren't you? The question is, what do you think you should do?"

Robert considered his options, based on the information he'd received from his new ally. He hoped they would be friends, perhaps for longer than everyone assumed they might.

"I think I might order a beer."

That week, Robert attended the studio meetings. He played the role of an experienced thespian and a grateful, enthusiastic visitor. They promised to phone him, but they didn't. He told them he was excited about their call, but he wasn't. Everyone parted on excellent, fraudulent terms.

A week after his return to England, Robert signed up for a play in the West End. He sent the comic four tickets for opening night.

Brotherly Love

A short story.

(I like my brothers. I'm a fan of the concept of siblings in general. None of the people in this tale are based on my relatives.)

A very rich man purchased a very expensive diamond. His finances were impressive enough that he could afford to buy it, but not impressive enough that he could realistically keep it. When it became clear that he had to choose between the stone he'd acquired and everything else he owned, he reluctantly debated his affection for each. Finally, after an argument with his children that threatened to rip the family apart, he arranged to sell it.

Eager to make a small profit and alleviate his disappointment, he talked up its beauty and increased its value. His statements attracted the attention of interested parties, including people who liked to bypass the monetary compensation aspect of transactions.

On the day of the sale, the diamond left the bank's secure vault under the owner's care. He carried it to three jewel cases, identical in all respects but colour, each capable of protecting it from damage. The cases were dark red, dark blue and black respectively.

He sealed the three cases with a combination that only he knew and passed them to his head of security without revealing their respective contents. The head of security placed each of the cases into heavy duty crates and locked each with a key for which there was no copies.

At two in the afternoon, the security team carried the three crates to three armoured vans for transport to the auction house. Each of the vans was under the control of an experienced driver from an established, expensive, transportation company. Everything that had happened to this point was according to the detailed plans of a brilliant, meticulous man.

Thirty minutes later, all three jewel cases were missing.

This is the tale of the people who stole them.

Lee and Ryan Beck were gifted and successful thieves who boastfully based their operations out of North Hill Court, a large stately home in several acres of countryside. The dilapidated property was old enough to carry substantial value, but remote and neglected enough to deflect tourists. Lee and Ryan lived at the house with Ryan's wife Violet and an elderly family friend called Thomas.

Oliver's younger brother Joe had escaped the family business and visited rarely. Although Joe committed as many crimes as any of his relatives, he'd consciously distanced himself due to his dislike for orders and his inability to settle in one location. He was a spontaneous and easily bored drifter, a charming and likeable con man.

Serena learned all of this from Oliver for the first time on their journey to North Hill Court. Prior to today, all she'd known of his family was his reluctance to discuss his family.

"I should have told you all of this earlier." Oliver admitted.

Oliver Beck was the odd one out. He had always been the good guy in a family that took pride in its bad guy status. As a teenager he'd struggled to fit in with the antics and misbehaviour of his brothers. Eventually, tired of his father's disappointment, he'd rebelled further and become a policeman. He'd excelled in the role, driven by his efforts to be the opposite of what his parents expected. He'd eventually become a detective who specialized in capturing criminals who reminded him of his older siblings.

"I know the circumstances aren't great ..." she said.

"They're really not great."

"... but I'm glad I get to meet them. We've been together for two years, we've been engaged for six months, and I've never met a single member of your family. They're important to you and you're important to me."

His smile disappeared a second after it appeared. Her kind words forced him to re-evaluate the wisdom of using her as cover for the visit.

"OK. You get your wish. You get to meet them. But, at the end of the day, you may get to see me arrest them."

Oliver took a photo from his jacket's inside pocket and passed it to her.

"I have something I can show you." he said.

Serena inspected the photograph from more than a decade before, an impromptu snapshot of three men. They each had the same fair skin and dark hair, but the similarities ended there. She guessed at which face belonged to which name, based on the descriptions she'd heard. Lee looked like an East End gangster from a Hollywood movie. Ryan looked like someone a movie gangster might send to intimidate a rival. The third brother in the picture was the youngest and the most handsome of the three.

"You look great in this." she said.

"You think so?"

"You don't? It's the best picture of you I've ever seen."

Oliver scowled, contrary to the reaction she'd expected.

"It's not me." Oliver admitted. "I took that picture. The man in the middle is my brother Joe."

"That's Joe?" she asked and looked more closely.

Embarrassed by her admission that her boyfriend's brother was more attractive than her boyfriend, she changed the subject.

"Maybe they didn't do it. Maybe they were here all day. Maybe your brother is ill, just as they claim."

"They may not have stolen the diamond, but Lee is up to something. Lee only falls this ill when he's up to something."

"He's done this before?"

Oliver laughed. He'd lost count of the times Lee had spread rumours that he'd reached death's door. He could ask Ryan for the number later. It might be a good conversation starter.

"My brother Lee is not a good person. If you forget everything else I tell you, remember that. Don't let his health fool you and be careful around him. He's the one person who doesn't care that we're family."

"You don't talk about the others as if they're much better."

"They're not very law abiding, but they love me, I hope. I can't promise the same of Lee."

Serena looked out the window at the beautiful countryside. It was a long drive and a world away from their small, cramped apartment.

"If I remember one thing, I remember that Lee's a bad guy. If I remember two, what else do I need to know?"

Oliver considered, compared and rated his possible answers.

"If Joe is there, don't play him at cards."

North Hill Court looked impressive from a distance, but careful inspection revealed its slow collapse. It looked much the same, but a little worse, every year.

Joe Beck climbed its steps with the widest of grins. He was home, finally, belatedly, and he hated this place. None of that dented the smile.

Thomas Maric, the apathetic man who posed as the building's butler, met him at the top of the front steps. What he lacked in actual job performance, Thomas presented regardless in traditional clothing appropriate to the role.

"Welcome home, Master Beck."

"Thomas, Thomas, Thomas. I didn't know how much I wanted to see you until I saw you. How are you?"

"My well-being is sufficient to sustain me through my limited contributions."

"Your eloquence is as inspiring as ever. What's the latest? Is my brother dying or is he faking it for deeply implausible reasons again?"

Thomas replied simply with a deadpan expression and no words whatsoever.

"What's his motive this time?" Joe asked.

"Everyone has a hobby, sir."

Joe grinned more enthusiastically. He'd forgotten how much he liked the old man, a fact he'd inadvertently buried under the memories of how much he disliked everyone else who lived here.

"We should catch up later." Joe said as he passed by and into the house. "We could play some cards."

"I will endeavour to be occupied every time you suggest it, sir."

The main foyer was grand and impressive. The staircase climbed ahead of each visitor and then swept around to both the left and right onto two parallel landings that led to the rest of the upstairs. The main floor included an impressive, period library and a rarely used billiard room on its left flank. A small lounge and a large dining room sat on its right.

The rear half of the house, narrower than the front and invisible from the main driveway, included a kitchen, a large storeroom used as a pantry, and a conservatory. The conservatory's windows looked out onto grounds that nobody tendered and a forest that swept around on all of its borders.

The upstairs had five large bedrooms and another five that resembled small cells. The largest of the former was the master, an imposing chamber that none of the Becks used because it had once belonged to their tyrannical father. The latter were servant's quarters near the rear of the house, a holdover from a forgotten era. This collection of tiny rooms bordered the steep, narrow staircase that dropped directly into the kitchen.

Joe considered his options and ventured left into the library. He knew they'd seen his approach. He knew they'd watched him arrive. They'd speak to him when they were ready.

Ryan's wife Violet was a tough, no-nonsense brawler during a heist, but unsettled and neurotic in the calms between storms. Ryan trusted nobody more during an operation. She made him nervous the rest of the time.

"Why is he here?" she asked.

"Lee invited him."

"Lee is unconscious twenty-two hours of every day and he frequently forgets his own name when he's awake."

"He told his brothers he was dying. That's an invitation."

"What do we do?"

Ryan thought through his options, as well as his wish to be out of his wife's presence.

"I don't know about you, but I'm going to say Hi to Joe."

The library carried floor to ceiling bookcases on two walls, interrupted only by doorways. The other two walls hosted tall windows and deep, wide internal ledges that beckoned to potential readers. The interior of the room included three oversized, antique chairs, two that faced each other conspiratorially and one that veered anti-socially towards the exterior wall.

Ryan descended the wide staircase, guessed Joe's probable location and found him in one of the library's antique chairs.

"Brother, I'm glad you're here."

"I came as soon as I heard." Joe replied. "Can I see him?"

"Maybe later. The nurse is with him at the moment. He'll be glad you're here."

"Will he?"

"The doctors say he's got a chance, but Lee's not convinced. He's started apologizing for things I never thought he'd admit. That's why I think it's real this time. Whatever happened between you, whatever was said, he'd want to see you. We'll check with Ursula later. She's the nurse."

"Ursula? Really?"

"Yeah. Like the Bond girl."

"Thank you, yes. Let's go with Bond girl. I was going to say evil witch from Little Mermaid."

Ryan appeared offended by the remark which Joe immediately translated as evidence of something else.

"Violet and I took your old room. If you need somewhere to crash, we can figure something out." Ryan said, steering the conversation elsewhere.

"I don't plan to sleep much. I'll use one of the cells above the kitchen if I need a nap."

"You're sure? ... Because that would be a great help. ... "

They looked up simultaneously as another car drove down the long, tree lined avenue towards North Hill Court. Thomas appeared in the doorway without warning.

"Your brother Oliver, sir." he announced.

"How can you tell that from here?" Ryan asked as they watched the distant car come closer.

"It appears to be a reliable and somewhat dull automobile, sir." Thomas said.

Joe and Ryan nodded, as if the explanation confirmed the theory.

A second vehicle entered their view. It had surrendered a head start to the first car, but it was gaining quickly. The roar of its engine drowned out the hum of the vehicle it followed. The music from its stereo reached the house before the laws of physics and considerate volume suggested possible. Nobody asked Thomas for his prediction of who might be driving the speeding car.

"You should warn Violet." Joe suggested.

"You may be right." Ryan replied.

Violet had freaked at the arrival of a brother. She wouldn't respond well to a visit from Ryan's ex-wife.

Oliver parked his car near the home's main steps and behind Ryan's BMW. All of Serena's attention was stolen from the old house they'd approached by the sports car speeding towards them.

"I think you should go inside." Oliver told her. "Stay in the library until I join you. It's the first left after the main door."

"What's happening? Who is this?"

"It's Natalie." he replied, without elaborating.

Serena followed his advice and walked into the house she'd learned of four hours earlier.

The black sports car skidded to a perfect halt alongside the BMW and her slide spattered a hailstorm of tiny stones into Ryan's car. A door opened and a woman with movie star beauty climbed out gracefully. It was a spectacular entrance from someone who excelled at them.

It would have been the simplest thing to fall in love with her at that moment. The reason Oliver didn't was because he'd fallen in love with her fifteen years earlier and he still considered it the dumbest mistake of his entire life.

"What is she doing here?" Violet spat at her husband.

"I need you to calm down."

The suggestion was pointless. They both knew that this was as calm as she was likely to attempt.

"What is *she* doing here?" Violet repeated.

"I don't know." he admitted. "If I had to guess, based on historical precedent, I would guess she's here to insult us, threaten us and then steal from us."

Violet grabbed Ryan's collar violently.

"Make ... her ... go away."

Ryan shook himself free of her grasp.

"She didn't listen to me when she was my wife. What makes you think she'll start now?"

Violet looked out the window at the expensive car, the expensive clothes and the beautiful woman who'd married and abandoned her husband. Violet had stepped into the role Natalie had discarded and she'd suffered the comparisons ever since. There was nobody she despised more in the whole world.

"Maybe you should tell her you love her." Violet mocked. "That didn't stop her from leaving last time."

The detective walked slowly towards Natalie, battling a collection of conflicted feelings and hoping to resolve them before he reached her. The slim chance he had of achieving this faded the moment he heard her voice.

"Hello Oliver."

"Natalie Wiley, what brings you to my day?"

"I heard about Lee's ill health. I came to pay my respects."

"Your respects? That's not really appropriate, in a lot of ways."

"Why? Because I hate him, because I divorced his brother, or because he's not really dying?"

"Choose any of the above. They're all good reasons."

She took his arm and allowed him to escort her to the house. She glanced upwards at a bedroom window and tried to suppress a smile when she realized who was watching.

"It's good to see you. I didn't know you would be here." she said.

"If I admit it's good to see you too, do you promise not to read too much into it?"

"I can't promise. Best not to say it."

"... I'm here with someone." he stuttered.

She brought their journey to a brief pause and released his arm. She inspected Oliver's expression and tried to decipher all the emotions he hadn't figured out for himself.

"Does she deserve you as much as I do?" Natalie asked.

Oliver hesitated. By most criteria there was nobody more amazing than the woman in front of him.

"… She's the most incredible person I ever met who doesn't kill people for a living." he replied.

Natalie produced a fake, sulky expression that didn't convince anybody.

"You say that and it makes me cry a little."

"I'm sorry. That wasn't my intention." Oliver apologized.

"Do you ever wonder what would have happened if I hadn't foolishly switched my attentions to Ryan fifteen years ago?"

"Do you think you would have done something other than kill people for a living?"

"… I don't know, but for you I might have killed a few less."

"That line wouldn't work from anyone else, but it may be the sweetest thing you've ever said to me."

She leaned towards him and whispered a response that left him more conflicted than ever.

"You never gave me a chance to say anything sweeter."

She took his arm again and they entered through the main door. Thoughts and dreams swirled around his mind more than ever.

Serena loved reading. She circled the room, her eyes fixated on the bookcases and the thousands of books the shelves supported. It was the most incredible room she'd ever entered.

She didn't see Joe at first. He'd claimed the high, wide chair that faced towards the window. When he spoke, he accidentally startled her and she stumbled into an endearing, childish giggle.

"I'm sorry. I didn't know there was someone in the room."

"There usually isn't." Joe explained. "It's one of the reasons I like it so much."

She recognized him from Oliver's picture.

"You must be Joe."

"It's a pleasure to meet you." Joe replied. "I have no idea who you are, which I already consider unforgiveable."

He switched to a different chair and invited her to take the oversized seat opposite him.

"Oliver didn't tell me much about you either." she said as she sat down. "I'm Serena."

"He is as cautious as I am indiscreet. If you have questions, I promise to be an invaluable and mischievous resource."

"I can ask anything?"

"Anything."

She looked around at the amazing room and then back at her future brother-in-law.

"This is going to be an interesting evening."

Ryan returned from his argument with his wife and intercepted Oliver and Natalie in the main foyer.

"Welcome to my humble abode."

"Your abode's not that humble." Natalie corrected.

"And my welcome's not sincere. What are you doing here Natalie?"

"Whatever I wish, Ryan, whatever I wish."

Since simultaneously quitting Lee's gang and divorcing Ryan, Natalie had become a very successful contract killer. This gave her license to act spontaneously with limited opposition around people who knew how she made a living.

Oliver looked between them. He was eager to see how the conversation would develop, but his conscience demanded he find Serena.

"I'll leave you two to … catch up."

Neither of them responded and he drifted sideways into the library.

He heard Serena laugh as he entered the room, a genuine response to a story Joe had confided, but an unfortunate welcome to a new arrival.

"I came to check." Oliver said. "I was worried."

"I'm fine." she said happily. "I met Joe."

Oliver crossed the floor, Joe stood up and the two brothers hugged. It was likely to be the final happy reunion of the day.

"Thanks for looking after her."

"It was my pleasure. Congratulations on your engagement."

Joe reclaimed his chair. They all heard raised voices from the foyer.

"There's been ... a development." Oliver said. "And it's one I should probably explain."

Joe took the hint, excused himself courteously and ventured through a door on the far side. He disappeared into the billiard room beyond, granting the couple some privacy.

Oliver wanted to confess his mistake, but he waited until Joe had closed the door. He spent these seconds considering how he might explain Natalie and wondering if that was even possible.

Natalie's arrival changed everything and he didn't want Serena here for whatever it had become.

"I should never have brought you here." he said.

"I wanted to visit. I offered to visit. And I like everyone I've met so far."

"That's because you met Joe. Everyone likes Joe when they meet Joe."

"Then what is it? Is it the woman in the sports car?"

Oliver laughed nervously and looked towards the foyer. He still didn't know how to explain Natalie. It was possible he never would.

Natalie broke from her argument with Ryan and joined Joe in the billiard room. She adopted the top of a long, wooden cabinet as a makeshift seat. Joe continued calmly with a game of his own invention, a hybrid of snooker and pool, as if Natalie's arrival was a perfectly normal development.

The billiard room included a full size table and all the necessary equipment for a game none of the residents understood. The pictures on the walls portrayed ancestors of the home's former owner, a collection of serious, military gentlemen. Each painting's subject suggested bravery, toughness and an inability to smile. The same faces had looked disapprovingly on those attempting to play games in this room for more than a century.

"Ryan wants me to leave. He thinks I'm a complication." she said.

"Think of yourself as an unexpected development. It's the same implication, but they're nicer terms."

"What about you? Do you want me to leave?"

"If you suddenly feel compelled to kill everyone in the house, do you promise to let me live?"

"You know I'd never hurt you Joe."

"Then, for what it's worth, you have my vote."

She curled her legs under her and admired the peaceful view.

"What do you know about what your brothers are planning?" Natalie asked.

Joe stopped playing to consider the question

"I know less about their plans than you think."

"OK. What do you think?"

He sighed, thought through the available evidence and provided his summary.

"They paid the three drivers and switched the crates before the vans were hit. They paid the drivers using the money they got from the three gangs who hit the three vans. I heard somewhere that their usual buyer retired, so they'll be working with someone they don't 100% trust, which will scare Violet into greater paranoia than usual. Lee is almost certainly not dying, which means he doesn't want to share, and chaos will ensue when they all try to double-cross each other. ... Oh, and Ryan is probably sleeping with Lee's nurse. What do you think?"

"More or less the same." she admitted.

"When will you make your play for the cases?"

"In the chaos that ensues when they all try to double-cross each other."

"Too lazy to search the house?" Joe asked.

"It *is* a big house." she replied defensively.

He nodded in agreement. She returned her attention to the view and he resumed his game.

Arthur Beck's old bedroom sat at the very front of the house. His sons had avoided it during his lifetime because he'd terrified them. They'd avoided it since his death because it reminded them of someone they preferred to forget. The resultant neglect inflicted on the room had seen it fall into disrepair faster than anywhere else in the building. It was a dark, sinister space, even without the bad memories it evoked.

It was bordered on each side by Oliver and Joe's old bedrooms. In response to his latest health issues, Lee had stolen Oliver's former room. Ryan had claimed Joe's the day after without explanation.

Since this switch, Violet had spent more and more of her time in her new room. It kept her within brief walking distance of Arthur's abandoned chamber, a neutral ground for everything in which Violet, Ryan and Lee had an equal share.

The three-way split worked most of the time, but there was always the unspoken assumption that it would fall apart one day if the prize was large enough. She knew that Lee and Ryan both expected this. She expected it too.

Violet was more anxious than ever. She'd already entered into the kind of panic in which she specialized between a theft and a sale. Natalie's arrival had amplified all of her concerns.

Ryan returned to the room and tried to reassure her unsuccessfully.

"We're out of here tomorrow morning." he reminded her. "The buyer will arrive and draw everyone's attention. While they're focused on selling, we'll already be running. They won't know we're gone until we're gone."

"You promise?"

He paused and attempted a confident, persuasive expression.

"I promise." he replied.

Denny, Oliver's partner, set up his base of operations in the woods. He was a short drive from North Hill Court, behind enough trees to leave him invisible to anyone not specifically looking.

There was still no word from Oliver when Morecombe, a senior detective from a local precinct, arrived, uninvited, to take over. There wasn't a single good reason for him to assume control beyond politics and geography.

"I read the file." he said rudely and repetitively each time Denny tried to question his involvement.

The file described how three different gangs had stolen three cases and how three different sources had suggested these cases were empty. There was a single enquiry looking into the drivers and a possible hand-off prior to the raids, but there were a hundred different theories as to who might have the diamond. It was Oliver Beck who'd suggested his brothers.

Morecombe engineered his way to the nearest vantage area and then moved closer to make a point. He intended it as a symbol of authority. Denny accepted it as a sign of poor judgment.

Eight more policemen from the local precinct arrived in the following minutes and solidified their control with their greater numbers.

"It is important, for the success of this operation, that I become more actively involved." he announced to Oliver's partner. "I want your recommendations for how we can arrange that."

Denny, whose every word he'd interrupted in the previous five minutes, delivered a rebuke instead.

"We don't know if they're responsible yet. If they are, Detective Beck is our best chance to confirm that."

"That would be the same Detective Beck who decided to run a surveillance operation without warning the local branches of his intentions? That would be the same Detective Beck who initiated this entire investigation based solely on a hunch?"

Oliver's partner didn't reply. He had no interest in a debate with Morecombe about pleasantries and protocol.

"Find me a role to play." Morecombe said. "Find me a role or pack up and leave."

Thomas retreated to his private quarters. It was a small, simple room that held a bed, his clothes and little else. He took a phone from his waistcoat and typed a short text message to the buyer. The new arrivals made the situation riskier, but Thomas had his own reasons for moving ahead regardless.

He dispatched the message and then switched to a website that discussed the value of very old books.

"Do you know why Ryan left his car on the driveway?" Natalie asked. "It's because they have building supplies and tunnelling equipment in the garage."

She'd peppered Joe with unsolicited information and thoughtful questions since her arrival, but this was the first statement to surprise him.

"You arrived two hours ago and walked straight into the house. How do you know what's in the garage?"

"I drove loudly down the driveway two hours ago. I arrived before that."

Joe considered the new evidence.

"... All of the vans were hit by professional gangs. All of the thefts involved trucks and guns and fast getaways. None of the thefts involved tunnelling."

"Hmm. Makes you wonder what the tunnels are for."

"And where they are."

"Oh, no." Natalie said. "I can guess where they are."

Her eyes drifted slowly towards the floor. Joe accepted her clue, but questioned her conclusion.

"No, I don't buy it. There's no way they're building tunnels and there's no way any of them would walk down a tunnel that any one of them had built."

"This is an old house." Natalie suggested. "What if the tunnel was already there? What if all they had to do was repair and strengthen it?"

Joe considered her question.

"... Then, maybe, they'd walk down it, if they had a good reason."

Natalie and Joe both knew the reason.

Ryan slid silently into Lee's room. He sat quietly alongside his sleeping brother's bed. Ursula, Lee's nurse, sat alongside Ryan and rested her head on his shoulder.

"I want this to be over." she whispered.

He turned to look at her. She was short and pretty, shy and quiet. She had almost nothing in common with his wife, a characteristic he found increasingly appealing.

"We get out of here tomorrow morning." he told her. "The buyer will draw everyone's attention. While they're selling, we'll already be running. They won't know we're gone until we're gone."

He didn't mention that he'd used similar words to reassure his wife.

"You promise?"

"I promise." he replied.

Their patient released a deep breath and they watched his eyes carefully for signs that he was waking. The moment passed and Lee continued to sleep.

"My younger brothers want to look in and I want to make sure that Lee's unconscious when they do. When would be a good time?"

"He should sleep for at least another hour. Now is as good a time as any."

"Thank you. I'll get them."

He kissed her and then kept kissing her, for longer than he intended, for longer than his excuses to be in here might explain. It was Ursula who eventually pulled away.

"Before your wife looks for you." she explained.

He nodded and went to find Oliver and Joe.

"I should fall in love with you next." Natalie said. "None of the others are any fun anymore."

Joe laughed politely.

Natalie broke from the shot she had lined up and stared at her former brother-in-law. She twirled the billiards cue in her hands until she held it like a club.

"Do you want to explain the little, involuntary giggle you just surrendered?" she said.

She slapped the stick into her other palm menacingly and then twirled the cue back into something less threatening as her smile returned.

"I would never date you and you know the reason why." Joe told her. "You are amazing and you will always be amazing. You may be the most amazing woman I would never date in the whole world."

"That's the nicest thing anyone has said to me all day."

"Well, it's early. You haven't pointed a gun at anyone yet."

"Compliments don't count if you have to point a gun to prompt them."

"That won't stop you trying."

"You're right," she said. "but that's because it's fun, not because they count."

Ryan, Oliver and Serena entered the room.

"We can see him." Oliver explained.

Natalie politely declined the invitation, despite not receiving one. Oliver, Serena and Joe followed Ryan out of the room and up the stairs. They followed the curve of the staircase and arrived outside their brother's new room. Joe glanced briefly at his father's bedroom, the one he'd avoided as a child, and he wondered about the new sleeping arrangements.

Ursula, their brother's nurse, opened the door for them. She asked them to be quiet and then retreated into the background. Oliver, Joe and Serena approached the bed, while Ryan hovered near the door. They left the curtains closed and the room stayed in shadow for the duration of their visit.

"Serena, this is my brother Lee." Oliver introduced.

Serena waved politely, but instinctively kept her distance. The eldest brother was still an intimidating figure. Far from looking peaceful, he looked menacing, even while unconscious. He'd recently shaved his head and the look was new to his two youngest brothers.

"I think he suits it." Joe whispered.

"I agree." Oliver said. "It's less of a Sherlock Holmes nemesis Mark Strong and more of a Rock'n'Rolla gangster Mark Strong. I think he pulls it off."

Serena looked between the two brothers, horrified by their lack of concern.

"Remember what I told you." Oliver whispered. "He's probably not sick."

"Although, you have to respect the effort this time." Joe added.

Oliver agreed.

They stayed with him for fifteen more minutes before deciding to end their visit. They left the room, conflicted on how much credibility to grant his illness.

Joe, Serena and Oliver visited the kitchen to review the dinner options. Each in turn found Thomas, the enthusiastically idle butler. The first to arrive was Joe.

"How is Master Beck, Master Beck?"

"He's quiet." Joe answered. "I'm so used to him shouting at me, it threw me off from our usual conversation."

"It is possible that he is dreaming of shouting at you, if that is a consolation, sir."

"It isn't, but thank you. What culinary delights do you have for guests Thomas?"

"I regret to inform you that it is the cook's day off."

"You have no cook."

"In keeping with the grandeur of our surroundings, I prefer to suggest that we do, but that she has many days off. Perhaps you might be interested in selecting something from the variety of options in the freezer."

Joe opened the door to the tall, stand-alone freezer and found a large collection of meals for one.

"Microwave meals? This is a celebration, Thomas, a family reunion. It hardly seems like a microwave meal kind of evening."

"As you well know, I am as committed to the preparation of food as I am to preserving the building's structural integrity and the careful maintenance of the gardens. However, if Master Joseph is disappointed with the cuisine, perhaps he could soften the blow by using the finer crockery."

Joe grinned.

"I might do that."

Oliver escorted Serena into the kitchen. They greeted the butler and joined Joe at the freezer. Despite Joe's comments, neither brother was surprised by the available selection.

"Do they have anything in a fake potato?" Oliver asked.

Joe handed him a shepherd's pie.

"Is there any real food?" Serena asked.

"No, but it looks like they have some spicy curries that might disguise the origins of their contents."

"OK. I'll take one."

Joe passed her a red Thai chicken and claimed a lasagna for himself.

"Nothing has changed in here." Oliver marvelled. "This kitchen's exactly as I remember it."

"On the contrary, sir." Thomas corrected. "I think you'll find that in support of the occasions when the residents wish to eat at similar times, we have purchased an additional microwave oven."

Violet decided to eat in her room, a petty act of isolation that surprised nobody. Ursula claimed she needed to monitor her unconscious patient. Thomas reluctantly took each of them some food at Ryan's request. After completing these tasks, he returned to his kitchen, his dinner and his determination to complete the minimum number of duties.

Natalie skipped the meal entirely and opted to stay in the billiard room for the evening. In an effort to avoid both his wife and his ex-wife, Ryan followed Joe, Serena and Oliver into the dining room. He brought no food and instead carried an expensive bottle of scotch and a glass. He poured himself a generous double and sipped at it slowly for the remainder of the night.

The dining room was the perfect illustration of the building's former greatness and its present state. It was dominated by a table that ran for most of the length of the room. It was too grand for North Hill Court's occupants, few of whom ate in here regularly. Its spectacular fireplace was unusable due to a seal they'd applied to block a persistent draught. The landscape paintings that displayed local landmarks were the works of talented artists, but the frames held onto the dust of every month they'd escaped appreciation or attention. Everything else that littered the room had outlived any potential value.

Oliver and Serena took the seats nearest the hall. Joe sat opposite them. Ryan claimed the head of the table, a decision whose significance nobody acknowledged.

The conversation started awkwardly, which Serena pretended to ignore by concentrating on her inconsistently heated food. They all tried to disregard the occasional flashes of light from the edge of the grounds, perhaps consistent with a small police team who'd strayed a few feet too far from the forest's tree line.

"I hear your career is going well." Ryan said.

He accompanied the compliment with an unimpressed tone that cancelled out any of the sentence's goodwill.

"I heard the same about you." Oliver replied.

Joe laughed briefly. He had the ability to find humour where no one else did.

"We know you disapprove of us." Ryan continued. "We know that's why you kept your girlfriend away until now, but it didn't have to be that way. You probably don't realise how much you hurt father when you left."

"Oh no, I know." Oliver replied. "He phoned. He told me. I don't remember him saying he was hurt though. As I recall, he went with some other words."

Serena, the only person who approximated to a neutral, tried to introduce a new topic.

"Oliver told me that this isn't the first time Lee has almost died."

The three brothers exchanged shocked glances and then erupted into laughter one by one. Despite their brother's ambiguous condition, his fake deaths were a reliable family joke.

The room feel quiet again, its occupants momentarily united. Oliver glanced at Serena and realized that she'd done this on purpose. He quickly persisted with the topic, something they could all discuss without controversy.

"How many is it?" he asked Ryan. "I couldn't remember."

"... That's a good question, and it's tougher to answer than it should be. I was talking with Violet the other day. She was talking about the fifth time he did it. There was only four I told her. We went back and forth a few times before she persuaded me. It turned out I had completely forgotten about his third fake death. She had to describe it for me."

"Ryan, you have a beautiful home." Serena said.

It was another subject she thought would be safe.

"Thank you. I'm glad you like it. I love this place and I wish we could look after it better. It's difficult."

Serena didn't understand the connection and Oliver provided explanation.

"Because the house is so old, they can only make changes using certain materials, even if the changes are necessary repairs. That makes it very expensive."

"We have no choice but to let it fail around us." Ryan added.

They all glanced around at their surroundings, a key room of the wonderful, dying building.

"Can't you use cheaper materials?" Serena asked. "Wouldn't that be better than nothing?"

"That would be illegal." the three brothers muttered in unison.

They smiled at each other. As children they'd frequently spoken the same words at the same time because shared experiences had prompted each with the same answers. It hadn't happened in a long time.

Some lights flickered from the edge of the grounds. Nobody mentioned it, but it clearly irritated Ryan. Oliver changed the subject again.

"Our father bought this house with money from his ... from his ..."

"Professional enterprises." Joe suggested.

"Thank you. ... He used money from his professional enterprises. To varying degrees, the family has co-owned it with various banks and creditors ever since. After our father died, Lee inherited his share. That's the short version of how a man obsessed with death acquired a house that reminiscent of a murder mystery board game."

Serena looked down at the table, but Oliver caught it.

"You've only been here four hours and you noticed already."

"I didn't like to say anything." she admitted.

"Don't be embarrassed. It has a library, a billiard room and a conservatory. It's not a giant leap."

"It even has secret tunnels." Joe added.

Oliver coughed loudly and Ryan almost choked on his drink. They were distracted from Joe's troublemaking by a brighter, longer blast of light from the woods. Ryan placed his drink down, walked to the window and looked towards the trees as it finally diminished.

"Do you know what I think of when I consider the words *incompetent* and *detective*?" he said. "I think of that game. I think of the characters from Clue."

"I thought it was Cluedo."

"It's Clue in America, Cluedo in Britain."

"Whatever it's called," Ryan said. "that's what I think of and it's because the detectives are idiots. They find a body. Then they spend forever trying to identify the murder weapon because they can't tell the difference between a strangled neck, a knife wound and a blow to the head. And even though they know that one of the others is the killer, they split up to search the spooky house for clues. They split up! That's their strategy. That seems like a good move to them."

He looked directly at Oliver.

"The killer could have a gun. They know that's at least a possibility. Why don't they realise how badly that game could end?"

Ryan took a short swig of his scotch and Oliver took the opportunity to respond.

"Those are all good comments and very well thought through, but do you know what I think of when I consider the words *incompetent* and *criminal*? I think of the same game. The culprit, let's say its Professor Plum, commits a crime. He then instantly forgets what he's done. Not only does he stick around, but he helps the others *solve the mystery*. Everything he does helps to prove his guilt. Ultimately, he can lose the game, despite knowing the crime's other details, because he hasn't worked out that *he is* the bad guy. So, when I think of incompetent, that's the guy I think of."

The awkward tension returned to the room and to everyone except for Joe.

"... No, I have to disagree. I have to defend the Clue murderer." Joe said. "We have to consider the possibility of conscious intent and genius. Think about it. It really doesn't matter what Peacock, Scarlet and Green think happened. Nothing they find will be admissible in court. I can hear the judge now, asking them about how they wandered the house, playing detective and tampering with evidence. The Clue murderer has been killing people for decades and he or she will never spend a day in jail if there's a half-decent defence lawyer."

"It sounds like you want him to get away with the crime?" Oliver asked.

"It's not about choosing sides." Joe answered sincerely. "Sometimes a winner is the player who deserves to win."

Oliver and Joe stared at each other, trying to read the other's mind.

"I remember a game I played with my sister when we were young." Serena interrupted. "We got something wrong during the set-up. We finally solved it and Colonel Mustard had killed someone with a dining room."

Oliver looked at his future wife and the microwave meals they'd placed on the expensive china. His smile returned.

"I think we all understand how that might happen." he said.

Detective Morecombe watched the house, desperate to know what was happening inside. Oliver Beck's partner stayed further back, in better cover from the pouring rain. He quietly pondered the probable failure of their surveillance's supposed discretion and Oliver's probable reaction.

As it approached midnight, someone from Morecombe's team crept forward to update their colleague.

"What is it?" Morecombe asked ungratefully.

"We intercepted a call. A woman, we think Violet Beck, phoned her cousin. She isn't happy about the visitors. She doesn't trust her husband. And she doesn't like that they're dealing with a buyer they've never met."

"Did she mention the diamond?"

"No."

"Then how do we know what the buyer is buying?" he complained.

A few spots of rain landed on their shoulders before progressing to something heavier a minute later.

"Do we have a name?" Morecombe asked.

"The buyer's called Novak."

"And they've never met him?"

"They've never met him."

After their late dinner finished, they gathered in the foyer. Ryan continued his conversation with his brothers, but took the opportunity to confirm Natalie's location. He spotted her in the billiard room, her attention on an old, classic book she'd borrowed from the library. His suspicions allayed, he made his apologies and retreated upstairs to speak to his wife.

Instead of going to sleep, Serena wanted to return to her inspection of the book shelves. Oliver encouraged the idea, but pulled Joe to one side after her departure.

"I need to go somewhere. I won't be long. Will you keep an eye on Serena for me?"

"I promise." Joe replied.

"Don't play her at cards."

Joe grinned and shrugged ambiguously.

"Please Joe. I need this favour." he begged.

"It's trust me or trust one of the others."

"OK, good point."

Oliver collected his jacket.

"When you check in with them," Joe whispered. "let them know they're too close to the house."

Oliver nodded sadly.

Ryan entered his bedroom to find his wife staring towards the intermittent lights.

"It doesn't matter that the police are in the woods." he told her. "Let them stay there. Let them get drenched by the rain. Nothing has changed."

"You would think that." Violet said, clearly unconvinced.

"We stick to the plan. We leave in the morning."

She glanced at the phone and thought about her recent conversation. Her cousin had reassured her too, but she couldn't admit that to Ryan because she'd promised not to make any calls.

She could see all of her options and plans and timelines. She saw how it could all go wrong just as clearly.

"Would anyone like a game?" Natalie offered from the doorway that connected the library to the billiard room.

Serena and Joe declined. Natalie politely left once more.

"What can you tell me about her?" Serena asked Joe.

"Natalie? ... Natalie is the most incredible, beautiful, very bad person I've ever met."

"Do you love her?"

Joe laughed.

"Why do you ask?"

"It's the way you smile when you talk about her."

"With someone like Natalie, the question is never 'do you love her?' but 'why doesn't everyone?'"

Serena hesitated before asking the question for which she really wanted the answer.

"Does Oliver love her?"

Joe stumbled over his answer uncharacteristically.

"... He ... That's ... "

He collected his thoughts and restarted his answer.

"Maybe a little, but there is something important to remember about Natalie and Oliver. They could have been something and Oliver is the reason they weren't. They didn't make sense then and ithey make even less sense now because she's done some very illegal things and he's got you. Natalie turns heads, so forgive Oliver if his head turns, but when she's leaves the room, he'll be with you."

"I think you'll find that she just left the room ... and he's not here."

"Which is bad news for my metaphor, but it's great news for me."

"The way you smiled just then makes me wonder if you love me a little."

"We only just met ... but maybe."

Oliver arrived at their makeshift camp as the torrential rain finally subsided. He inspected the developments and breathed a sigh of relief.

"I was scared that my closest colleague had tragically lost his intelligence and professional ability. Thankfully, he doesn't appear to be responsible for any of the horrible decisions made since I entered the house."

He looked at Detective Morecombe as he said it and any chance of collaboration ended immediately.

"The only reason your investigation is still underway is because I permitted it." Morecombe replied.

"The main reason the investigation you've permitted to continue is a complete embarrassment is because you're too close to the house. They're going to see you if they haven't already, which is my polite way of saying that they already have."

"Your family are thieves, not psychics. Don't give them too much credit."

"They're very good thieves. Don't give them too little credit, or do you want to compare the house they live in to yours."

Their conversation degenerated from there. They quickly descended from a disinterest in cooperation to an enthusiasm for sabotaging the other.

"I found some cards?" Joe said as he lifted a deck from a nearby bookcase. "Would you like a game of something?"

"Oliver warned me not to."

"My absent brother has predicted and foiled my evil plan."

"Perhaps you could show me a trick instead." Serena suggested.

"I could do that."

Joe shuffled the deck quickly, impressively. He asked her to pick a card, look at it and return it. She did so. He shuffled the cards again, faster than she could follow.

"Do you remember your card?"

She did.

"Are you happy with your card?"

She was.

He shuffled the deck again and slyly produced four cards, facedown, from his sleeve.

"So? What's my card?" she asked.

"Oh, I have no idea, but here is what I pulled from the deck in case you agreed to play me at poker."

He turned over the cards to reveal the four aces. Serena laughed.

"I wish we'd met before." she said.

"That's very kind of you, but it's also dangerous. Are you happy?"

"Yes."

"I'm glad. And I want you to understand that's there's a connection between your happiness and this family's absence from your life. Oliver kept you away for a reason and it's a good reason. The more time Oliver spends with his brothers, the more he gambles with your future."

"I didn't mean the whole family." Serena corrected. "I only meant you."

"Oh. ... That's OK then. Spending time with me only gambles with your future a little."

"We're sending them a buyer." Morecombe explained.

"A buyer? Who?"

"Me." Morecombe confirmed. "They have a name and not a face. I will be that face."

Oliver assessed and dismissed the plan immediately.

"... but it will never work. We know nothing about the buyer."

"We know your brothers haven't met him. That's good enough for me."

"This is a dumb stunt because you want to be in the middle of this. You can't take chances with my family."

Morecombe turned to his colleagues.

"If he tries to contact his brothers or approach the house, arrest him. If he resists arrest, restrain him."

Morecombe's colleagues nodded their understanding. Oliver's partner avoided eye contact.

"My fiancé is in that house." Oliver reminded Morecombe.

"Yes, she is. You probably shouldn't have left her there."

Thomas returned to the kitchen. He set the kettle boiling. It would be a long night and his long night needed some caffeine.

It was forty years, almost to the day, since Thomas's first encounter with the notorious and talented Arthur Beck. Over the years, Thomas had acted as getaway driver, lookout, alibi and trusted friend. With the father's death and the family business in the hands of the two eldest sons, he'd transitioned to a new role as fake butler and unwanted tenant.

He served a household of four brothers and the only one of the four he liked didn't live in the house. Joe's short-lived return had only served to remind Thomas of his mixed feelings for the Becks and how his most negative views concerned the two eldest brothers. His loyalty to this family was over and the repayment of their debt to him wasn't as final as they thought it was. Everything from the situation to the complications of visitors to the deteriorating weather told Thomas that his near future should involve retirement to somewhere warmer than the wet, English countryside.

He checked his messages. The buyer was on his way.

Ryan sneaked into Lee's room. Ursula silently showed him the tablets she planned to give Lee that would send him into a longer, deeper, harmless sleep. Ryan smiled his approval and kissed her.

He looked at Lee one more time and day-dreamed about finally emerging from his brother's shadow. A confrontation between them had grown more likely with each passing year. It was time for them to part ways. It was time for Ryan to step out from the shadow and prove that he was more than Lee's sidekick.

It was his time to shine, but he was happy for Lee to sleep right through it.

Violet pulled a shoebox from her closet and discarded its lid. She took out two guns, checked they were loaded.

She walked quickly and quietly to the front bedroom, the one they'd abandoned and neglected since Arthur Beck's death. She stepped inside and closed the door behind her.

It was a massive room, filled with grand, large furniture. Every item was covered in a sheet and a subtle wave of air from an unidentified source lifted each sheet slightly. In the dark, it added to the room's reputation of a ghostly presence.

Violet lifted one of the sheets, hid the two guns in the top drawer of a nearby cabinet and replaced the sheet.

Unable to resist, she approached another tablecloth and another cabinet. She looked underneath at the three cases trapped between the furniture and the floor. Joe and Oliver's arrival had cost them their opportunity to smash the locks and look inside. Until they did, the cases themselves remained the most captivating mystery she'd ever seen.

Her eyes moved between each case and wondered which held the diamond. She selected dark red as her favourite, disregarding blue and black from her consideration on a gut feeling. She decided that when she finally escaped this building, the red case would be in her grasp.

Natalie discreetly tip-toed out of the billiard room and into the foyer. She confirmed that nobody was in sight and then edged up the stairs. She glanced in every direction to confirm her journey remained a secret, but her eyes kept returning to a bedroom door, the bedroom nobody liked, the bedroom nobody used anymore. It was central. It was neutral. And she instinctively knew were the cases were.

She completed her climb and crept slowly along the corridor that led to the back of the house. She'd located the diamond's hiding place. Now she wanted the tunnel.

"You must have someone." Serena said.

"Why do you say that?" Joe asked.

"I don't want to answer that."

"If I promise to withdraw the question, can I accept it as a compliment?"

"Yes, I'd like that."

"... There is someone," Joe answered. "but it's not going to work out."

"How do you know?"

"She likes me as a friend, as someone who is helping her family. But it's not the same as how I feel about her, and that's why staying with her wouldn't finish happily for me."

Serena trusted his judgment and didn't question it further. She glanced into the next room on impulse and confirmed that Natalie wasn't there.

"Where do you think she is?"

"She's probably looking for the jewel cases my brothers stole." Joe replied.

Serena's jaw dropped before she could control her response.

"Natalie told me she'd wait for my brothers to make a move, but I guess there's no harm in looking to pass the time. I understand the impatience."

She thought about pleading ignorance, but decided against it.

"You know about the diamond?"

"I know about the diamond. More than that, I can guess where the cases are. Nobody trusts anybody in this house and everybody's changing bedrooms in the same week. That's too much of a coincidence and two and two make four. They've stashed the cases in the haunted bedroom nobody sleeps in because they're scared by their memories of our father."

"Are you here to steal it?" Serena asked.

"No. Stealing isn't my thing."

"What is your thing?"

Joe paused before replying.

"... I would say my thing is proving I'm more intelligent than everybody I know who thinks stealing is their thing."

Natalie descended the steep steps into the kitchen and found Thomas in the chair he'd occupied for the majority of the evening. She looked around the room for possible entrances to the tunnel. She noticed some inconsistent patterns in the wood behind his chair.

"Can I help you with something, Miss Wiley?"

She took a seat on the bottom few steps and pulled out a cigarette. She wordlessly requested permission to light it and Thomas granted it by lighting his own.

"I always liked you Thomas. You know a great amount, but you say very little of any consequence. It's a combination I always found intriguing. Let me ask you a question. What do you think he sees in her?"

"Are we discussing Master Ryan and Miss Violet?"

"No, Thomas. Nobody is discussing Miss Violet."

The butler smiled.

"I have not spoken extensively with the young lady, but she's seems ... nice."

"... I'm more interesting."

"If you'll pardon the expression, miss, you may be too much of a good thing."

"What do I focus on in that sentence? Am I a good thing or too much?"

"You may choose either miss, if it stops you from staring at the wall behind my chair."

"There's one thing I still don't understand." Serena said. "You're not here to say goodbye to Lee because you suspect he's faking. You're not here for Oliver or Ryan because you're hardly spoken to them either. You're not here for Natalie because you didn't know she would be here. And you're not here to steal the diamond because ..."

"Because?"

"... You told me that isn't the reason and I believe you."

"Maybe it was to meet you."

"You didn't know I would be here either."

"You're right, but it was a happy coincidence and Oliver is a very lucky man."

"Thank you," she replied, embarrassed. "but you didn't answer my question."

"Yes, but you almost didn't notice that."

She stared at him and waited.

"You were almost right the first time." he confessed. "I came to say goodbye."

"... It's you. It's you that's leaving."

"I don't know when I'll be back. If you still want to invite me to your wedding after today, I probably couldn't attend. I'm sincerely sorry about that."

"This woman, whoever she is, you really love her, don't you?"

"Yes, and it's time for a new start in a new place with new, gullible victims. And I'm happy to say that gullibility doesn't limit my possible destinations. But, please, don't tell anyone. I don't want this visit to be about me, not even for a minute. It's going to be more fun if it's all about them."

"Fun?" Serena said. "Is that what this is?"

"It's there." Joe answered. "You have to look carefully, from an angle, with an open mind."

The conversation in the library continued into the early morning. Ryan and Violet Beck decided to forego sleep because they both mistrusted at least one person who'd opted to stay awake. Natalie kept to herself in the billiard room. Ursula stayed in Lee's room to monitor her patient. Thomas remained in the kitchen and kept a watchful eye on the entrance to the tunnel they'd carefully rebuilt.

The buyer was due at seven. Morecombe scheduled his arrival for six.

An hour before his arrival, Serena finally slipped into unconsciousness, despite best intentions. She dreamt about searching the house for Oliver, unsuccessfully, and finding only people looking for diamonds.

Ten minutes before Morecombe arrived, Ryan was the first Beck to close his eyes.

The doorbell woke Ryan from his brief sleep and he momentarily forgot where he was. At some point in the previous minutes, his wife had left the room. He hadn't heard her exit.

Natalie raised her head slightly, but betrayed no other emotion. Nothing surprised her anymore. She was ready for whatever might happen, whenever that might be. She always was.

Serena snapped to attention. She immediately looked around the library for Oliver and found only his younger brother. Joe smiled as she looked up and gestured for her to stay in her seat.

Thomas walked slowly across the foyer and reached the entrance as Morecombe rang it a second time. He opened the door slowly.

"I'm here to see Ryan Beck." Morecombe said. "He's expecting me."

"Please step in, sir."

Morecombe entered into the spectacular foyer. He thought back to Oliver's taunt and spontaneously compared the house to his own. The comparison wasn't pretty.

He waited politely while Thomas closed the door and then turned to face him.

"I'm delighted to be here. My name is Novak."

"I know." Thomas replied. "You're my nephew."

Thomas pushed a black device into the policeman's side and Morecombe collapsed as the electricity tore through his body.

The butler gazed down at the unconscious detective.

"... You look different somehow."

Oliver and Denny watched events from the cover of the trees. Morecombe's colleagues, in a continual defiance of common sense, occupied the space their supervisor had claimed nearer to the house.

"This might end badly." Oliver said.

"For you family or for Morecombe?" his partner asked.

"It might end badly for my family. There's no way this doesn't end badly for Morecombe."

They watched the silent house. There was no obvious movement. There was no news, good or bad.

"If I hear a single gunshot, I'm running for the house." Oliver said. "And I'm knocking down anyone who tries to stop me."

Ryan arrived half-awake, confused, into an empty foyer. He looked at the closed front door and then spun around in his search for answers. Thomas returned to the foyer and Ryan appealed for an explanation.

"I heard ... I heard a ... "

"You heard someone arrive, sir. It was the buyer"

An expression of panic spread across Ryan's face.

"We're not ready for him. I'm not ready for him. This complicates everything."

"If you will forgive the unfortunate news, the situation is further complicated by the buyer's change in height and his sudden ability to speak English."

"Police?"

"The gentleman is unconscious and unable to confirm that, sir."

Ryan hesitated. He registered these new developments, considered his next steps and then dashed up the stairs. His instinct took him not to the diamond, but to the person he hoped would join him when he took it. He sprinted into his brother's room in search of Ursula. He looked towards the table where she had left his brother's modified medication and it was gone. He checked below a mountain of bed covers and found his brother's nurse, a million miles away in a safe, deep slumber.

He took two steps backwards as his dazed brain processed the unexpected events and then ran for the haunted bedroom. He instinctively drew a gun from the back of his jeans and walked in on his brother and his wife withdrawing three jewel cases from underneath disused furniture. Each of them turned and pointed a gun in Ryan's direction.

"Going somewhere?"

"Thinking about it." Lee replied.

"It's a good day for it. You're looking better."

"Thank you. I feel better."

Ryan continued to aim at his brother, but his eyes flicked towards his wife. He tried to recall clues of her betrayal and came up with nothing.

"You've spent your whole life trying to be your older brother and never quite achieving it." she explained. "I realized I was settling for the replica when I could have the real thing."

He ignored her and the dangerous impasse persisted.

"There are three cases and three of us. We take one each." Lee offered.

"That's a two in three chance I get nothing. I don't like the odds."

"I don't like your odds right now."

Ryan didn't see Natalie appear in the doorway behind him.

"This could get messy." Ryan told his brother.

"It will get messy." Natalie said. "Not a one of you can shoot straight."

Serena stepped back into the library and carefully closed the door.

"What do we do?" she whispered.

"I suggest we stay in the library." Joe replied. "If there's a gun battle, they're unlikely to flee in this direction. If there isn't a gun battle, none of them are big readers anyway."

"This wasn't your deal, Natalie." Lee said.

"Any deal is my deal if I decide it is. It's a luxury I grant myself because I *can* shoot straight. I want one case."

"We don't know which one holds the diamond." Ryan told her.

"I'll take my chances. I'd need two hands to carry two cases and I'm not ready to put my gun away yet. I'll take one case, whatever its contents, as payment for walking away."

"And if we say no?"

"I shoot you all for free."

The brothers considered her offer, much to Violet's horror. Natalie continued to hover on the edge of the doorframe, her weapon held discreetly behind her back.

"There's three of us and one of her." Violet reminded them.

"Yeah, we'd need at least another two people." Ryan replied.

After a few more awkward seconds, Lee kneeled down slowly. He slid one of his two cases to Ryan and Ryan pushed it to Natalie with his foot. Its outer shell was black.

"A pleasure doing business with you all again." she said happily.

"I really wish you'd never brought that woman into our lives." Lee complained to Ryan.

"And so says the man who persuaded my wife to point a gun at my head."

Violet looked at the case and the woman stealing it. She thought about raising her gun and debated it against how much she wanted to instead of the likelihood of its success. She made her decision, but the weapon never reached the height of her shoulder.

Natalie fired once and then ducked around the corner. She threw herself to the floor and stayed low as the standoff imploded. Violet fell backwards with Natalie's bullet in her arm, striking her head on furniture as she fell. Ryan and Lee took aim at each other and emptied their cartridges at the opposing wall, finding their target through probability instead of skill.

The brothers slid to the floor on opposing sides of the room, bleeding onto the wooden floor with multiple, non-fatal wounds. They stared at each other and carelessly allowed their guns to slide from their hands. Holes decorated every square metre of the walls behind them.

They'd finally committed to the confrontation they'd dreamt of for years. All they had achieved was an inconclusive, agonizing draw.

Natalie edged along the wall silently. She picked up the black case and walked to the staircase. She passed Thomas on the steps and nodded politely. He nodded in return.

Thomas entered into the bedroom and inspected the damage. Ryan requested assistance in the loudest voice he could manage and delivered only a whisper. Lee attempted the same and produced even less.

Thomas ignored their requests and stepped towards the dark blue case that rested by Lee's feet. He located the red case by Violet's body, but he couldn't see where her weapon had landed. He decided against approaching her.

"I was hoping that you would all commit to this predictable, overdue falling out and leave. After you'd gone, I was going to gather and sell the contents of the library. I think that would have worked for everyone. Unfortunately, I recently applied an electrical charge to someone who might be a police detective and I have to allow that to influence my short term plans."

He calmly collected the dark blue case and abandoned the room.

Natalie located the tunnel behind Thomas's seat in the kitchen and fled the house within a minute of the first gunshot. Thomas followed the same path soon after. He carefully closed the entrance behind him and exited at its far end before the police discovered its existence.

The policeman created a makeshift perimeter around the house. Oliver and Denny approached the front door and waited for a signal.

"Library." someone shouted. "She's in the library."

Oliver sprinted inside with his partner in pursuit. He glanced briefly at the staircase and then ran to the left. Serena and his younger brother sat inside, quietly discussing recent, probable events. She stood up as she saw him and he ran into her arms.

"I should never have brought you here." he whispered.

"I was never in danger." she replied.

Joe smiled and stood from his chair. He slid the pack of cards into his pocket and the four aces into his sleeve.

"So," Joe asked, "do you have somewhere we can make a statement?"

A dozen detectives streamed into the house from the front and back. They discovered Morecombe bound and gagged in the pantry. They found three injured people amid the chaos of an upstairs bedroom. They woke a groggy, confused nurse. They recovered one of the three missing jewel cases.

Ambulances arrived.

Witnesses departed.

Nobody died.

And then they opened the cases.

The dark red jewel case completed its journey to the auction house under police escort. The owner's head of security met them there. A crowd of people surrounded him as he entered the code and released the lock to reveal an empty compartment. The owner had opted not to attend after learning the case's colour.

Thomas Maric released a slow, deep breath. He smashed the hammer into the chisel and the lock flew across the room. He repeated this for the second lock. He released another deep breath and lifted the lid. It was empty.

He laughed, because he'd already, cynically, predicted its contents. He had decided that, despite each event's equal probability, Natalie would have the diamond. Fate favoured people like Natalie. None of the day's events had persuaded him otherwise.

Natalie sipped at her drink and nibbled on some food in her expensive hotel room. The case remained locked and closed for several hours. She didn't need to check the contents because she was already convinced that she'd stolen the right case. Thomas wasn't the only one who believed that fate favoured people like Natalie and she had a lifetime of evidence to support the theory. She checked with a contact and confirmed a possible resale price, a sum that would support her expensive lifestyle for several years.

Still glowing from the victory over her former husband, Natalie disabled the locks on the case and looked inside. It was empty.

Her smile faded and she continued to view it, hoping for a clue to whatever mistake she'd made. She wondered if the police had recovered it. She thought about the possibility that Thomas had secured it for himself. She second-guessed her decision to not attempt a recovery of another case.

Finally, she thought about Joe. She recalled their evening and everything he'd told her and she realised he'd outsmarted her. She didn't know how, but he'd outsmarted them all. She smiled and she kept smiling.

"We will have words, Joe Beck." she muttered to herself. "We will have words."

She didn't plot anything more violent. She was too impressed to be angry.

A very rich man purchased a very expensive diamond. His finances were impressive enough that he could afford to buy it, but not impressive enough that he could realistically keep it. When it became clear that he had to choose between the stone he'd acquired and everything else he owned, he reluctantly debated his affection for each. Finally, after an argument with his children that threatened to rip the family apart, he arranged to sell it.

Then he met a criminal who explained how keeping both might be possible after all. The criminal offered his services for a very respectable fee, partly for the money but mostly because he was in love with the rich man's daughter. Eager to make a small profit and alleviate his disappointment, the rich man advertised the sale. The criminal ensured that this news reached the right ears.

On the day of the sale, the diamond left the bank's secure vault under the owner's care. He carried it to three jewel cases, identical in all respects but colour, but carefully dropped the diamond into his own pocket. He sealed the empty cases with a combination that only he knew and passed them to his head of security. The head of security placed each of the cases into heavy duty crates and locked the crates.

The security team carried the three crates to three armoured vans for transport to the auction house. This was all according to the detailed plans of a brilliant, meticulous criminal.

Thirty minutes later, all three jewel cases were missing.

The criminal followed the empty cases to the home of his two oldest brothers. It was to be one, final visit before a long trip of indeterminate duration. He watched his family fight over the empty cases, a turn of engineered events that provided perfect entertainment for his stay.

Joe looked once more at the check he'd received for his services. He would send some to Thomas because the old man deserved some good fortune. He would send some as a peace offering to Natalie and hoped she might not kill him in return.

He would also send an anonymous engagement present to Oliver and Serena. He hoped they would be happy. Recent events and probable convictions improved their chances.

By the time he'd distributed his newfound riches there would only be enough to cover the initial costs of his relocation. That didn't trouble him. Joe hadn't done this for the money. At least part of his motive had been to win a game he'd forgotten to tell his brothers he was playing. That kind of dishonest trickery is allowed when your thing is proving how smart you are.

There had always been an unstated contest between the four brothers. It was over and Joe was its unofficial victor.

Sometimes, a winner is the player who deserves to win. Sometimes, the best way to win is to pull the best cards from the pack before the start of the game.

Dodos

A poem.

Do dodos drive Datsuns with dirt on the dashboard
 or Daimlers with dents in the doors?

Do dodos do dentistry, drilling the dentures,
 or do they dig ditches in floors?

Do dozens of dodos drift daily to drink,
 drink drams 'til they drop or they die?

Do they drop in the ditches they dug in the day
 or dodge them and drop close nearby?

Did daredevil dodos do dangerous duties
 and deeds which due death defied?

The daft Dodo denizens don't do these duties.
 The dodos don't do them. They died.

And Eric Bana

A short story.

"I think I've worked out my superpower." he said.

I didn't reply. I knew it probably related tangentially to Martin's unsuccessful pursuit of fame and fortune. Unfortunately, my silence didn't discourage him; it rarely does.

"Every journey needs a first step." he continued. "I haven't made my first step. That's why I haven't started my journey and that's why I haven't completed it. I haven't reached my goal of fame and fortune and it's your fault."

I responded. I should have stayed silent, but I responded.

"How could *your* failure to reach *your* goal be my fault?"

"I asked myself that same question and it was my answer to that question that revealed my superpower. Everyone has skills and apparently mine is the ability to blame you for any and all problems in the world."

"Really?"

"Test me."

"I really don't want to."

"That's OK. Let's cut to how it could and should work. You become famous. They make an award-winning drama about you. I am everyone's favourite character in your story. I get the best lines, I get And status, and Eric Bana plays me in the movie."

"And status? What is that?"

"Good catch. We must obey the rules that control the opening credits and I must have And status. The main characters get top billing. The rest of the cast appear in order of diminishing importance. Then, suddenly, the coolest actor gets And status. And Jack Nicholson as The Joker. And Robert DeNiro as The Godfather. And Eric Bana as me."

"It's a good choice. He's an excellent actor. But you are aware that you don't look like Eric Bana?"

"It's artistic license. Ben Affleck doesn't look like Tony Mendez. However, it is important that Eric Bana plays me so that even if the film is a disappointment, which we know is possible, my reputation would survive the critical onslaught."

"You mean like with The Hulk."

"Very much like The Hulk. I liked the bits with Eric Bana. I hated almost every bit with the Hulk except for the tank spinning I'd already seen in the trailer. Something is very wrong with a Hulk movie when the best bits are the bits with no Hulk. And I give Eric Bana most of the credit for what was right."

"It's a fair point."

"And then there's Troy, the dumbest Brad Pitt movie that isn't Legends of the Fall."

"My ex-girlfriend loves Legends of the Fall."

"Everyone's ex-girlfriend loves Legends of the Fall. Everyone's ex-girlfriend loves Troy too. They love it so much that they overlook the absurdity of the central romance. Boy meets girl. Boy kills all of girl's co-workers. Boy kidnaps girl and protects her from bad people that she's only at risk from because he kidnapped her. Girl starts to like boy, which suggests she is surprisingly forgiving of the whole co-worker massacre incident. Boy starts to like girl and releases her to the safety of the city he is about to help burn to the ground. Boy then leads the assault against the city in the hopes of rescuing the girl from the city he recently released her to and dies in the attempt. Girl is heartbroken, which confirms she was surprisingly forgiving of the whole co-worker massacre incident. In the midst of all this mess is Eric Bana playing one of the few likeable characters. Troy is immediately a better film if it defies history, literature and overwhelming, Greek military resources and lets the Trojans win. That's what Eric Bana can bring to a movie, even when the movie has as many problems as Troy. He's a safety net. He's my safety net. Eric Bana is my defence against the possible awfulness of a movie about you."

"Who plays me?"

"I don't care as long as it doesn't distract from Eric's portrayal of me."

"You've given this plan a lot of thought."

"I have and it's perfect."

"Your less-than-perfect plan has a big problem."

"Is that the part where you haven't accomplished anything of sufficient importance to justify an award winning drama about your life?"

"That would be the problem, yes. And until I do ..."

"My failure to achieve fame and fortune are your fault. I can tell you're impressed. What can I say? It's my superpower."

The Stubborns

A short story.

Adam was a communications and mediation specialist with expertise in international politics. He'd worked with governments, agencies and corporations to reach consensus on complicated, contentious issues. He'd spoken with presidents, kings, despots and probable, future saints. He'd worked in cities, jungles, refugee camps and war zones.

It was difficult. It was challenging. He was very good at it.

However, when people learned what he did and the abilities these activities required, they didn't ask him about his experiences. Instead, they asked him to listen to their arguments.

It is for this reason that Adam didn't tell most people what he did for a living.

He didn't lie when asked, but he provided insufficient information for accurate determination. His on-going struggles with this issue were due to an all-too-common social quirk known as Free Diagnosis.

The most famous example of this habit, and the reason for its name, is the instinct among many to ask off-duty doctors for medical advice. Other examples include asking mechanics about car problems, interrogating stock brokers for tips and expecting chefs to provide appetizers to every gathering they attend.

For some people, it is a seamless transition from learning a stranger's occupation to requesting their assistance. It's an immediate expectation. The problem is that most professionals complete so many working hours in a typical week, they don't want to practice that profession in their spare time.

Adam loved his job, but it was stressful. Away from work, he actively pursued hobbies that included almost everything available to him that didn't resemble that work. Unfortunately, when some strangers learned his profession, they would try to enlist his help. To avoid these requests, he downplayed his fascinating career. He'd discovered the hard way that it was best to say as little as possible about his exciting life.

The best example of his struggles with Free Diagnosis was his unfortunate dealings with Ralph and Enid Steuben, a couple routinely referenced behind their backs as the Stubborns.

The Stubborns could argue about anything. More than that, they *liked* to argue about anything. They were desperately in love, and yet their consistent failure to agree on anything appeared to be the foundation of their relationship. This insanity worked for them, but it was a nightmare for anyone drawn into their world.

The following incident is a good example of Adam's interactions with the squabbling couple. It is not the first time Adam met them. In all probability, it won't be the last time he meets them. This is the story of the first time he encountered them after distributing specific instructions to all their mutual acquaintances to not invite him to anything the Stubborns might also attend.

Adam received his first warning the moment he entered the apartment.

"I'm really sorry." the host said, without prompting, without explanation.

"No?"

"Yes."

"No!"

"Yes."

"Stubborns?"

"I invited you. My wife invited them. We forgot to compare lists."

Adam slid his arms back into his coat, the same one he'd slipped from his shoulders twenty seconds earlier.

"What are you doing?"

"I'm sorry. I can't be here."

"You have to stay. My brother-in-law agreed to attend specifically because I promised you would be here. He wants to talk international relief projects and nobody but you will understand his acronyms."

"It won't matter." Adam replied. "None of it matters. If the Stubborns see me, they'll recruit me as the umpire in one of their ridiculous debates and no one else will have a chance to speak to me. There is no escape from their fights. The

Stubborns are Alcatraz to a pleasant evening's San Francisco; I can see the city, but I can never get there."

"Maybe they won't this time. ... Maybe? ... OK. Maybe they will."

"I have negotiated peace treaties. I personally brought peace to a land that had fought for centuries before my arrival. They kept that peace for 59 days and that's a personal best for a region that excels at responding disproportionately to decades-old differences of opinion. The people there lived for two additional, unhappy months because I made it possible. That was me, I did that, and I am not and never will be a marriage counsellor for crazy people."

"I know and I'm sorry. All I can offer is that maybe they won't."

The host slowly slid Adam's coat off his back and out of his guest's defeated grasp. Adam closed his eyes, as if the disappearing coat represented something more ominous, perhaps fatal. The two men entered the main room together.

"Adam." a voice shouted. "Adam, we need you."

Adam's host sighed and abandoned him. Adam reluctantly drifted towards a pretty couple in the far corner.

"Hi, Ralph."

"Adam, you're the only one who can help us. We need someone to resolve this once and for all."

"Not someone, Adam." Enid added. "We need you."

Adam nodded his consent. He'd tried refusing before, but disappointment and resultant complaints were one of the few things that united them. If there was one thing worse than the warring pair, it was the same couple unified.

"These are the ground rules." Adam told them. "Four arguments per person. One minute limit for each argument. No interruptions during the other person's turn. No shouting. No swearing. No attempts to injure or kill the other person, the impartial adjudicator or any passing, innocent civilians."

They look offended by the rules, as if breaking one would never have occurred to them. Adam continued.

"At the conclusion of the debate, the judgment is final and everyone leaves the discussion for a cooling period of thirty minutes."

"Is it usual to have a cooling period whose length exceeds the discussion?" Enid asked.

"Circumstances dictate conditions. I must insist on it."

He didn't expect them to obey the rules, but it was worth a try. In his most ambitious dreams, he still hoped to escape their grip and rescue part of his evening.

"The difference of opinion concerns a family, a very successful family." Ralph explained. "They have two individuals who have excelled beyond all expectations. Enid and I disagree on which of these individuals deserves the most praise and recognition, from both inside and outside the immediate family."

"Is that an accurate opening statement?" Adam asked.

"Yes, that's accurate." Enid replied.

Adam took no consolation from their initial agreement.

"This will go ugly fast." he predicted under his breath.

He glanced around the room for something he'd previously missed that might offer an opportunity for escape. He saw nothing that suggested freedom and reluctantly started the debate instead

"Enid, your first statement. One minute limit. Go."

"My first statement? She came first. She paved the way. We don't know that she explicitly supported his early career, but we can safely assume that she did. He has achieved a great deal, but would he have achieved as much without her early support? We don't know either way, but possibly not. She can take all the credit for her own achievements and some of the credit for his."

"I dispute that." Ralph interrupted. "She brought him to a wider audience, but fame is independent of success. He could still have achieved a great deal in obscurity."

"No counter-arguments Ralph." Adam cautioned.

"Sorry. Yes."

They both looked at Enid.

"... He completely broke my train of thought."

"Ralph, your opening remarks. Please expect Enid to respect the interruption guidelines as strictly as you did."

"That's unfair." she said. "I haven't interrupted him yet."

"Do you plan to?"

"I don't know. Maybe."

"Then it's only unfair until you do. Ralph, your opening remarks."

"Haircut."

"Really." his wife interrupted.

"And now it's no longer unfair." Adam mumbled.

"He has a cool cut. She looks two dimensional. If you met him in real life, you'd instantly question him about his interesting life. If you met her, you'd take one look at her haircut and forget everything you wanted to ask."

"You want to judge two incredibly successful cousins on their respective haircuts?"

"I don't want to, but that's how bad her haircut is. We don't have a choice."

"Enid, your second argument."

"Her friends love her for who she is." she said, ignoring her husband's immediate scoffing. "His friends like him because he does stuff for them. That seems fair-weather to me. You wonder if one day, his friends will wake up after a bad night's sleep and reconsider the relationship. Her friends know that there is nobody like her. His friends know that if they lose him, there are other family members who'll take his place in a heartbeat. She promotes more love, more devotion, and more loyalty. She has lifelong friends. He's just a useful guy to have in a pinch, surrounded by moderately grateful hangers on."

Adam looked at Ralph for his response.

"That was ludicrous. I don't know where to begin."

"That's good. Hold that thought. What's your second argument?"

"OK, truly, honestly, he saves lives. The *moderately* grateful masses my wife dismisses are grateful for his acts of bravery, heroism and, yes, lifesaving. That's what he does. What does she do by comparison? She runs errands. If I were her, I'd be embarrassed to discuss my day in his presence. What did she do today? Who cares? She didn't save lives. Why are we even comparing them?"

"Yes, why?" Adam whispered, before re-joining the discussion.

"Enid, your third argument."

She took a deep breath, as if she regretted the steps her husband had forced her to take.

"I didn't want to do this, but as you are devaluing *true* friendship, I think we have to look at best friends. Her best friend is reliable, helpful and funny. He will always be by her side and he will always be reliable, helpful and funny. By comparison, we have to consider the possibility that when *his* best friend grows up, his best friend will most likely eat him for dinner."

"That is ridiculous." Ralph shouted. "Take that back."

Adam stepped between them and deflected Ralph's outstretched arm from grabbing his wife's collar.

"I didn't say it would happen." Enid added. "I said it's possible. I think that's a genuine risk when your best friend is a baby jaguar."

This was the moment when Adam realised that the argument he was embroiled in concerned children's cartoons. He despaired more than usual for his lost evening.

"Ralph. Please offer your next statement." Adam said.

He didn't want to hear the next argument. He wanted to hear all the arguments and then walk away.

"Explorer is a cool job, but it's much cooler when you're exploring places that no one has been before, which isn't the case for her because Map always knows the way. And let's face it, half the time she's going to Tallest Mountain. It's kind of embarrassing she doesn't know the way by now and still needs Map to help her out. He claims to be an animal rescuer and he backs it up by rescuing animals. She claims to be an explorer and she backs it up by getting lost on a weekly basis."

"Enid, final argument."

"She has a backpack. He has a rescue pack. At face value, the rescue pack is more useful, but the song it sings goes on for an eternity. One of these days, he'll need a parachute and die tragically waiting for it to arrive because his rescue pack is still singing. The back pack can't turn into anything, but nobody will die because of an inability to be appropriately efficient in a crisis."

"Ralph, final argument."

"… I'm stunned." he admitted. "I don't know what to say."

"That's the nicest thing you've said all day."

"But let me say … let me say … Rescue Pack can turn into anything. Anything! I'm stunned you included that as one of your arguments."

"Ralph, is that your final argument?" Adam asked.

"Anything!"

"I'll take that as a yes."

Adam started to remind them about their agreement to the guidelines regarding the final decision and the cool off period. Before he could finish, the debate descended into a shouting match as the couple threw words as ammunition. They yelled terms like Swiper and Bobos, Fiesta and Click, Oh Man and Rosie Perez. Any hope that Adam retained of escaping their company started to diminish.

A woman joined them and hovered on the edge of the debate. She listened carefully to the latest round of accusations. As the argument paused, the couple and their mediator looked at her, a new arrival who'd inexplicably approached them by choice.

She was pretty and cheerful, slight and confident. Adam liked her immediately. He wanted to scream in her direction that it was too late for him but she could still save herself. She ignored his psychic warnings and spoke to them.

"I overheard your discussion and I'd like to contribute." she said. "I think I can offer something that might work for everyone."

She had their attention. She had so much of their attention that The Stubborns didn't interrupt her, an uncharacteristic turn of events.

"Our host has a guest room with a television, a DVD player and some of their daughter's old TV shows." the woman said. "Maybe one of the DVDs has additional evidence that could help to settle your debate."

The Stubborns loved the idea. They agreed with each other for thirty magical seconds and then argued about who liked the idea more.

They travelled as a group from their corner to a side room. As they passed through its doorway, the woman gently touched Adam's shoulder and he instinctively understood her request. He lingered in the doorway while The Stubborns began to inspect the DVDs and the woman set up the television.

She passed them the control and suggested they discuss which episode to play first. As the inevitable disagreement started, she exited the room and pulled Adam with her. The Stubborns argued for ten minutes before they realized they were alone.

Adam introduced himself and offered his thanks. The woman told him her name was Jenny.

She asked about his job and he told her the truth. He was desperate to impress her and share stories of adventure and danger that made his life sound incredible.

He asked about her job and she skirted around her answer. She eventually admitted that she didn't like to talk about her work and sometimes lied about it to avoid the requests for information that followed an honest admission. He understood completely.

She finally confessed her profession after he promised not to ask any questions.

Jenny was a hostage negotiator.

Very

A very short story.

It was a slow night, slower than most. George and Jay, the only occupants of an area that didn't boast any living residents, strayed to the other side of the stone wall and into The Widow's territory. It was a minor invasion of the kind that she tolerated because any response would involve talking to them.

They rested against the limited remains of the thousand year old structure and inspected the scene for something, anything, to distract them. Nothing arrived.

"I don't feel very." George said, without context.

"You don't feel very what?" Jay replied.

"I don't feel very, you know, very."

"I have no idea what you're talking about."

"I knew someone a long time ago, pre-death, pre-ghost, etc. He used the word dead to mean very, as in dead good, dead lucky, dead cool. It didn't bother me at the time, but now that I have more insight into the whole afterlife experience, it doesn't make sense to me. I know I feel dead, some nights more than others, but I don't feel very."

"It's not supposed to make sense. It's slang. Half of our language doesn't hold up to scrutiny."

"All the same, I think I should look him up, have a chat, and let him know that it doesn't make sense. I should point out some of its specific weaknesses as an expression and perhaps discourage its future use."

"Oh, is he dead too then?"

"No. ... I think on some level that's the reason my message will be more effective."

Bad Bet

A short story.

She was in fine form. She was persuasive, inspiring and intelligent. The newbie didn't stand a chance. He was smitten from the first minute. He was completely hooked by the end of her speech.

It's tradition to mess with the newbies using some means or other. Rarely had the means presented itself so obviously. I was completely confident in the method of my mischief and the method was Becca Lerman.

She was the most beautiful, most brilliant and most unavailable woman in the company. She never dated colleagues. She rarely strayed into non-work discussions. It wasn't simply that she was out of our league; she had consciously, deliberately excluded herself from any league in which one of her co-workers might be a participant.

My best friend Cal adored her. If anyone stood a chance, it was him. He's a great looking guy, a lot of fun and a terrific catch if you ignore his history of philandering and indiscretion. It was because of his failed attempts that I knew about her policy of not dating colleagues. It's because of his enquiries that I know the reason.

Becca met, dated and married a colleague at her first company. The marriage lasted two years and she left a promising role to more away from her ex. To the best of our knowledge, she instigated her policy soon after and she hasn't broken it since.

Her career recovered from that early inconvenience and she became the youngest and most gifted of the senior management team at the firm where I worked.

She's amazing. She was clearly far beyond the newbie's reach and I wanted to have fun with how little he knew that.

Did I mention that I'm not a good person? I think I missed that part. My apologies. I'm not a good person. I'm really not.

I spoke to Becca after the meeting because I owed her a report.

"You'll have it this afternoon."

"You said that yesterday." she replied.

She accompanied her criticism with a sweet smile. She has a skill for delivering rebukes in a way that people don't object to receiving them.

I admitted to my error without hesitation. It's better to be caught in a mistake than caught in a lie. A wise person told me that. You may have guessed already, but the wise person was Becca.

"I'm waiting on some numbers from Head Office." I explained. "I missed their office hours yesterday and I wanted to wait a cycle before calling today. It upsets them if we send them questions when it suits our time zone."

"This afternoon then." she said.

I suddenly wished that I worked at a different company because it might improve my limited chances with her. I had a sudden desire to reduce the number of reasons she would never date me from 7 or 8 to 3 or 4. She's very easy to adore.

I hesitated, long enough for it to be awkward and obvious, but then regained my composure.

"What do you think of the newbie?" I asked.

"I don't like him." she replied. "Keep him out of my way."

It wasn't like her to be so negative, but I respected her instincts. If Becca didn't like him, there was something wrong with him. If Becca didn't like him, he wouldn't last here.

"I thought he seemed OK." I said.

She opened her mouth, as if to argue, but her expression drifted into a smile instead.

"You're right. Everyone deserves a shot, right?"

"Right." I agreed.

I had the strangest sense that I didn't know to what I'd agreed.

"What do you think of Becca?" I asked the newbie at lunch.

Cal had arranged a small, select gathering that included the two of us and the newbie. I'd told Cal my plan and he'd signed on immediately. Did I mention that Cal is not a good person either? He really isn't.

'That speech was incredible." the newbie replied. "I came out of that talk ready to make a difference, desperate to make a difference. She's very ... I wish I could ...It was a great speech."

"She's beautiful too." Cal added, more bluntly than I would have liked.

The Newbie paused, perhaps suspecting a trap.

"I think what he means is that beautiful women have an advantage." I said. "We instinctively want to listen to them. They have that head start. But what's impressive about Becca is what she does with that head start. It's the ideas she brings. It's the work rate she brings. I know exactly what you mean about the affect she has on those around her."

The newbie agreed with what I said and I breathed a sigh of relief. I signalled to Cal and he politely bowed out of the conversation.

"Do you think you're settling in?"

"... Maybe. The guys are a bit cliquey. You've been great. You've been friendly. Some of the others, not so much."

"I can help there." I said. "They've got a bet going. If you get on board with it, that will score you some points with them. The best part is you don't actually have to do anything."

"What's the bet?"

"Becca won't date anyone from the company. First guy to get her to dinner wins."

He looked uncomfortable.

"It's like I said." I reassured him. "Tell them you're on board and if anyone asks you about it, tell them you're still working out your approach. And it won't matter that you'll fail because they all do. It's part of the deal. They all try together. They all fail together. There's a strange camaraderie to their collective failure."

"Are you in on it?" the newbie asked.

"I say I am, but I don't do anything about it. It keeps me in the conversation. It keeps me in the clique."

I could tell he liked Becca. I could tell he hated the idea. His consideration of the conflicting instincts lasted about ten seconds.

"I'm in."

I thought about it that evening and started to question my plan. I'd focused on the newbie and I still saw something amusing in his inevitable misfortune and embarrassment.

However, when I considered what might happen if Becca heard about the bet, I knew I'd made a mistake. I respected her and this wager sent the wrong message. I decided to speak to the newbie the next day and stop the prank before it went any further.

I missed him before work and a series of early meetings. I finally caught him in a corridor mid-morning after I heard a rumour he was looking for me.

"I was thinking the bet's a bad idea." I said casually. "You're new. You don't want to be a part of anything like that. Let's forget I mentioned it."

"Ah... that might be difficult." he replied. "That's why I needed to speak to you."

"What do you mean?"

"I won the bet. ... I mean, wow, I *really* won that bet."

I didn't believe him. It didn't make sense. Nothing about it made sense. I responded as eloquently as I could, which is to say with no eloquence whatsoever.

"You ... You what? ... How?"

"That's for me to know and you to ... It's for you to not know."

"But. But. But. Wait. OK. OK. Let's say for a second that I believe you."

"Which you don't."

"Which I don't, but let's say for a second that I do. How would I know that you were telling the truth?"

"That's a good question." he acknowledged. "I have evidence."

My brain flitted through all the possible explanations for his use of the word evidence. The newbie looked around conspiratorially.

"But not here." he said. "Let's go to my office."

I followed him to his office, a depressingly small unit with no windows that they always inflicted on the newest member of staff. I spent the entire journey trying to think of a reason to stop following him.

As I walked in, I saw Becca and Cal.

"For what it's worth, he had second thoughts and tried to back out." the newbie said.

"That *is* good to know." Becca replied. "Thanks for your help with this."

"You're welcome."

"I still don't like you." she added.

"I know." he said.

The newbie sensed that this was his prompt to sit quietly and he selected the corner nearest the door. I took the only available seat. It was next to Cal and across from Becca, but Cal didn't look at me. He appeared to be angry with everyone in the room. His anger appeared to disregard his previous enthusiasm for the scheme.

"You owe our newbie some money." Becca told me. "I'm not sure he cares about it, but you're going to pay him anyway. I will accept it on his behalf."

She waited patiently for me to retrieve my wallet and hand over the notes.

"Whose idea was this?" she said.

"It was mine." I admitted.

It's better to be caught in a mistake than a lie. A wise person taught me that.

"Then you'll be paying Cal's portion too."

I handed across some more notes.

"Now, as I understand it, and stop me if I get any of this wrong, you made a bet with a new employee and the bet was me. You challenged him to get me to dinner, but I suspect that is a euphemism and the bet was to get me into bed. And presumably, if all three of you got me into bed, whoever got me there first would win. Is that an accurate summary?"

I hesitated, long enough for it to be awkward and obvious.

"Yes, that's accurate."

"I know you like to have fun with the newbies, but this was the wrong bet with the wrong newbie. I would like you to apologize to him and then apologize to me."

I did, immediately, calmly, sincerely.

"How do we know he won the bet?" Cal asked.

It was a question that nobody should have asked ever. Cal left the company through mutual consent three weeks later.

Becca didn't blink.

"When did we first go to bed?" she asked the newbie.

"It was seven years ago." he replied.

"Seven years?"

"It was after your sister's birthday party. We were playing some weird game with vodka shots."

"Oh, that's right. ... *That* was a good party."

"I'm kind of hurt that you didn't remember."

"I'm kind of hurt that you divorced me, so be a good sport and get over it."

The newbie smiled and nodded.

Becca passed two pieces of paper across the table.

"What's this?" Cal asked angrily.

"Those are the dates and times of your respective visits to human resources to discuss practical jokes."

Cal grabbed the paper from the table and left the room without permission. I watched him go and then returned my attention to Becca.

"You have to know the mess you're in, but you're smiling." she said.

"I tell a lot of jokes." I explained. "It wouldn't be right to frown at this one, even if the joke is on me."

"I'm going to tell a lot of people this joke."

"There are a lot of people who'd like to hear it. I've had fun with the newbies for some time now and everyone has been one."

"Give me a good reason not to add this to your personnel report."

I considered a selection of reasons and decided that if good was a requisite characteristic, none of them qualified.

"Anything?" she said.

"No."

"Congratulations. That was the right answer."

She smiled as she said it, but accompanying the smile was her disapproval of everything I'd set in motion.

Unlike Cal, I stayed at the company, but I never climbed as high as I might have done. Reputations are tough to shake and I was forever the unfortunate fool who played the wrong prank on the wrong newbie.

The joke was on me and the joke was never old. It was a victory for the newbie and everyone has been one.

Duck

A poem.

Have you heard
 about a careless bird
 that went out one day
 and was blown away?

He waddled too far,
 passed a hunter's car.
 They didn't like his quack
 and they shot him in the back.

The moral is clear:
 from the path don't veer
 or you'll be main course
 in a chef's house sauce.

Better than Santa

A very short story.

A few years ago, my son decided that he liked Santa Claus more than he liked me. I thought this was unfair for two reasons. Firstly, Santa was taking all the credit for presents I had bought. Secondly, Santa doesn't exist.

Unfortunately, I couldn't use Santa's non-existence as evidence for my superiority in a conversation with a child who still believed in him. Instead, I nodded politely and admitted, reluctantly, that Santa has some good qualities.

However, the discussion sparked a debate in my head. Was this assessment reasonable? Was Santa better than me?

To determine, once and for all, whether this was true, I decided to compare myself to the red-jacketed, sizeable-bellied one in a collection of carefully selected categories. I would award points to the victor in each category. The eventual winner would be the recipient of the most points.

1) Popularity

I really wanted to give myself a point in this category under the basis of actual existence, but I can't because I don't have a problem with respecting fictional characters. Instead, I decided to break the tie by means of in-depth, well-considered science, and by science I mean Twitter.

Santa has several accounts and these cumulatively account for almost one million followers. I have significantly less and this total includes the people attempting to sell me Twitter followers.

That's an early lead for Santa.

2) Pets.

I strongly believe that the more unusual a pet is, the more interesting it is.

I have a cat who decides on a daily basis whether to acknowledge my existence. This isn't unusual. Lots of people have a cat who decides on a daily basis whether to acknowledge their existence.

Santa has reindeer.

Another point for Santa.

3) Flying Pets

This may seem like a very specific category, but it is such an impressive ability that failure to consider it would discredit the analysis.

The only way my cat can fly is if I place him in a carrier and load the box on a plane. If I do this, he will make me pay for it when I am least expecting his overly elaborate, feline revenge.

Santa's reindeer can fly. They can do this because they're magical.

I'll let that sink in for a moment and then award another point to Santa.

4) Pop Culture

Santa has appeared in books, movies and television shows. He also appears in poetry, including a very famous poem that identifies his reindeer as Dasher, Dancer, Prancer, Vixen, Comet, Cupid, Donner and Blitzen. You may recognize these names and you may know the poem I am referring to.

The reason many of you can identify his reindeer by name is that even Santa's reindeer are more famous than I am.

This score line is getting embarrassing.

5) Career

Picture the scene. You are attending a dinner party at a friend's house and you spend the latter part of the evening meeting the only guests you've never met before.

When we reach the subject of careers, I tell you that I publish books as an independent author. Santa tells you that he works for a charitable organization that distributes toys to tens of millions of children worldwide.

I can't compete with that. Two points for Santa.

And now that I've decided that multiple points are available in certain categories, I'm awarding him a bonus point for flying pets.

6) Location

This might be the only category I win.

I live in North America and in a climate that remains freezing for much of the year. As such, I understand how unpleasant the cold can be, but my summer gives me a break from these low temperatures.

There is no reason for somebody with Santa's money, power, fame and popularity to choose the North Pole as the base for his operations. While Santa's freezing off parts of his anatomy, I'm claiming the point.

This could be the start of a glorious comeback.

Probably not.

7) Vacation Days

Vacation days are an important perk to many of us because it affects our ability to spend time with our families and pursue our favourite hobbies.

Now, we would all admit that Christmas Eve must be tough on Santa. There is a great deal of work and the only reason he is able to achieve everything he attempts is due to magic.

However, after the Christmas season is over, he can delegate almost every other task to an elf work force on minimum wage.

Santa receives more than 300 days of vacation per year. 300! By contrast, I receive *considerably less than 300*.

That ends my comeback.

8) Free Food

I love free food. Thanks in part to Santa and the spirit of giving he promotes others to mimic, I do well for free food in December. It's still no contest and few of us are in the same league as Santa when we compare our snacks to his impressive haul.

If Santa gets one cookie at every one in a hundred houses, and that's a modest estimate, he still receives more than a million free cookies. No wonder he's larger than life. If you ate a million cookies, you'd be larger than life too.

9) Songs

Santa appears in some very catchy songs. You probably know some. Please don't sing them.

He also appears in some very annoying ones. You probably know some. Please don't sing them.

Appearing in songs is an impressive claim to fame, but appearing in annoying tunes isn't a sacrifice worth paying to achieve it.

I'm torn on this one and calling it a draw.

10) Power

Santa has a list. I'm reliably informed he checks it twice.

His list has a power over small, gullible children, including my son. I can only emulate this by telling my son about Santa's list. As a parent, I benefit greatly from my child's improved behaviour and his belated attempts to make the nice list. However, Santa is the true creator of the list, the true genius behind its power, and I give him due credit.

The final point is Santa's.

Final Result)

For those of you who kept track of the increasingly one-sided point totals, you'll know it is looking bad for me.

However, I have a final opportunity to rescue the debate. I am going all-in and betting everything on one final category, with winner takes all and Santa too fictional to dispute my controversial, last minute tactics.

The final category is my son.

Santa does something for tens of millions of the world's children, but I would do anything and everything for my son.

I am better than Santa, whether my son knows it or not, and no flying pets can ever change that.

What I Did When I Wasn't Saving the World (Prologue)

A novella.

I upset people. It's the easiest task in the world for me. It's so well known that I once attended a performance appraisal that suggested my ability to irritate others is the skill at which I excel more than any other. For some reason, I remembered this piece of critical assessment shortly after Carver pushed my head into the ground with the barrel of his shotgun.

You might wonder why I entertain these situations, knowing that these types of developments are a possibility. I confess that predicaments such as these aren't ideal, but I accept them as part and parcel of my work. And I love my work, mostly.

"Was it something I said?" I asked politely.

"Where is your friend?"

"He's not my friend. He's my employee. He's not here because I didn't need him and I told him I could handle this. Do you seriously have a problem with me arriving alone?"

Carver, my point of contact and the man debating the merits of my continued existence, paused before replying. I waited patiently for a temporary compromise or the loss of my head.

Carver removed the gun. I climbed to my feet and abandoned the kneeling position he'd demanded. I turned slowly, careful to appear unshaken and unimpressed. These were the two key personality traits of the fictional character I'd created for this assignment. Carelessly stepping out of character was one of the most dangerous mistakes I could make at this time. Fortunately for me, I'm unshaken and unimpressed most of the time anyway.

"I don't like you." Carver said. "I don't like your face and I don't like your attitude. And I don't like last minute changes to our agreement. Give me a reason to go through with this."

"We both know that there are nice people that don't have my attitude or my face," I admitted. "but I pay better."

Carver didn't reply because he knew I was right. He could dislike me as much as he wanted tomorrow, but the large amounts of money we'd discussed were a good reason to be here.

"You wanted a face to face with someone who doesn't give many." Carver said. "I've worked for him for a year and I've never met the guy. You insist, so, fine, I pass on the message and you get your wish. But after tonight, you send your friend. When we pay, send your friend. When we deliver, send your friend."

"You make a lot of demands for a middle man."

"I want this to go smoothly. Your friend makes that more likely than you. He doesn't make me want to jam a gun into the back of his head."

"And I do?" I said. "Well, I get that a lot."

I really do. It once said something similar in a performance appraisal.

We walked into the hotel's lobby. It was dirty, badly lit and deathly quiet. Paint peeled from the nearby walls and elaborate cobwebs nestled in every corner. It was an axe-wielding murderer short of a horror movie. My prospective clients were notably elsewhere.

Carver sighed. He wanted this meeting over as quickly as I did and their absence depressed him as much as it disappointed me. He checked his phone and received his explanation.

"They're running late."

"You need to give me more than running late because I do business in a lot of countries and the people I sell to don't run late."

"He says he was at a football game. The game's finished, but he's stuck in traffic near the stadium."

"I'm minutes away from making the biggest deal of his year and he kept me waiting to watch a soccer game?"

"It's an important game."

"Don't mix business and pleasure. It's a nonsense sport."

"Some people say football is a matter of life and death."

"Maybe we know more about life and death than those people."

The elevator arrived and we both stepped inside. As the doors closed, it occurred to me how unfortunate it would be if the antiquated machinery failed to deliver me safely to the top floor. It would be just my luck to die in a freak elevator accident.

The doors closed and the elevator I'd trusted with my life reluctantly moved upwards. I kept a straight face and held my tongue, but the 60 second journey scared me more than the man escorting me.

Carver was a stereotypical bruiser. His language sometimes hinted at an education, but his body shape suggested nightclub bouncer.

I was a little shorter, a little weaker and a little older by comparison. I hoped I was a little more intelligent, because he had the edge on me in most other categories.

The other difference between us is that although I spent a decade in England between the ages of three and thirteen, I am American. It's a trait that seems to antagonize most of the British criminals I encounter. I am aware that America has committed some mildly anti-social acts in recent decades, but I wasn't personally responsible for any of them. Being morally judged by thieves, thugs and killers, while initially amusing, got old a long time ago.

More than any other day I could recall, I was excited to return home. My short term plans included a flight from the criticism of the British shores and a return to the unappreciative arms of my fellow countrymen. I wanted to see my apartment and sleep in my own bed. I'd overstayed my welcome and it was time to go home.

"You wouldn't understand." Carver said as the doors opened.

I stepped out of the elevator quickly, half expecting it to plummet down the shaft a second later. It took me a few seconds to realize Carver's sulky expression was independent of our current business and connected to my dismissal of his country's national sport.

"Because I'm American? Please, explain it to me."

"Life can't be all work. We've got beer, women and football. It's what we do. What do you watch? Baseball?"

"Baseball is the sport of kings."

"You have no kings. We call it Rounders here and little girls play it."

"Guess who plays soccer where I'm from."

My phone rang as we reached a set of double doors. I excused myself politely, walked a few steps to the side, and then answered.

"Hello."

"It's a trap. Get out of there."

I exchanged glances with Carver. He was irritated by the interruption, but oblivious to the warning.

"I'm with someone. I can't talk right now."

"My cover is blown. That falls back on you. Get out of there."

"Thanks for the information."

I ended the call before my colleague could protest further.

"Problem?" Carver asked.

"Yeah, with my next deal, but next week's deal is next week's problem."

Carver opened the double doors and we entered into the room beyond. Once upon a time, it had been the most expensive suite, but it had since lost its furniture, its carpet and some jagged shapes from its internal walls. The window's still contained glass, but the rotten window frames let a steady breeze pass through anyway.

I looked around until I'd located all the possible exits. Before I could move towards any of them, Carver's phone rang. I waited patiently and watched his face for a reaction.

He greeted the caller, nodded a few times, spoke very little. It was possible he was receiving detailed instructions regarding the disposal of my body. He was six feet from my position and the entrance was four. I made a judgment call, took one step towards the door and he pulled a gun in response.

"Consider it done." he said calmly.

He placed his cell phone back in his pocket and stared straight at me.

"Your friend trashed your cover. They want me to kill you."

His honesty was refreshing. His apparent indecision on whether or not to actually shoot me was appreciated.

"Can we reach a deal?" I asked.

Carver threw me the gun, which I admit confused me.

"My name isn't Carver. My name is Evan Noah and trying to save your useless American life is going to cost me eight months of undercover work."

"I'm sorry. I didn't know."

"Save it. Your buyer isn't coming, but he will send friends."

As he said this, four cars stopped outside the window, several floors below us.

"You said trying to save my life." I said.

"What?"

"You didn't say you would save my life. You said you would try to save my life. It's a subtle distinction, but I was wondering if you were aware of it."

Noah removed a second gun from an ankle holster.

"I was aware of it." he admitted. "We won't make it out of the building."

He was wrong about that. Evan Noah, the man who started the evening by threatening my life, ended the evening by saving it.

At the centre of everything that followed is how I repaid him.

What I Did When I Wasn't Saving the World (Part 1)

I lay on the bed and stared at the ceiling. It wasn't a particularly interesting ceiling, but I can't get comfortable lying on my side anymore. It also hurts to move or to sit for too long. Lying on my back is the position whose continued adoption prompts the least amount of agony.

I've seen a lot of ceilings in the last six months. This is one of the consequences of my decision to jump from a third floor window in a hail of gunfire, bounce awkwardly on the roof of a passing truck, and land heavily on the road.

My doctor returned to the room.

I like my doctor. He's intelligent and excellent within his chosen field. He's also belligerent, argumentative and he doesn't tolerate my poor behaviour for longer than he needs to. He doesn't shy away from telling me when I'm making a mistake and he's more than capable of delivering his rebukes in a sarcastic tone that would infuriate some but entertains me. My family are sarcastic. I was practically raised by it.

He glanced at his notes as he collected his thoughts. It was an obvious stalling tactic. There was little in the notes he hadn't memorized.

"I read your service file last night."

"Don't believe a word. The version you have access to is mostly fiction."

"I'm conducting informal research into why the most professionally competent people make the worst patients."

"I'm guessing misplaced self-confidence."

"Yes, that was my conclusion too." he replied.

He sat near to my bed.

"For what it's worth, take it easy. You've ignored most of my recommendations, but I mention it in the hope you'll follow my instructions someday."

It was a legitimate complaint. I'd spent six months on a three month recovery plan because I didn't follow doctor's orders. I thanked him for the advice without promising to follow it.

"Based on these results, I'm authorizing your return to work." he said.

I didn't react. I accepted the good news and waited patiently for the bad news I was certain would follow.

"What are you going to do with your newfound mobility?" he said.

"I'm going to solve everything that's wrong in the world."

"That could take a while."

"I'll start with everything that's wrong because of me. That should only take about a decade."

"Nicholas, I'm only authorizing reduced level. You know what that means?"

It meant I was stationed behind a desk. I nodded and the doctor apologized. He understood what work like that did to people like me.

"Don't apologize." I said. "It wasn't you who shot me."

I shave intermittently. Previously, I took care with my appearance because I wanted to present a professional image. That's not necessary anymore because my fame goes before me. I'm Nicholas Hadley. I'm the man who walked into a building filled with gunmen wanting to kill me and then almost destroyed my body during my escape. The truth is more complicated than this, but I've discovered I can't control my own reputation.

Granting yourself permission to look like a vagrant is a very liberating experience. You can pretend that you're rebelling in your own small way. You can tell yourself that you're not conforming to rules and regulations. In truth, you're encouraging people who disrespect you to elevate the level of their disrespect. On the plus side, it saves you 10 minutes each morning.

The only reason I reference this neglect is that I still take more care with my appearance than my apartment. Hopefully this conjures an image of my home and saves me the trouble of describing it further.

Someone knocked at my door and I predicted it was Kit Jordan. I don't receive many visitors. I've discovered that many of my friendships operated within a specific radius of which I was unaware. My inability to travel to that radius regularly is sufficient for me to disappear from their plans and considerations.

Kit continued to visit for several reasons. He's my best friend, a job title he's owned for several years based on shared interests and a common sense of humour. It should also be noted that it was Kit who compromised my alias on my assignment in England. He's indirectly responsible for three of the seven disasters currently afflicting my life.

I walked to the door slowly. I walk everywhere slowly. I opened it to a slim thirty-something. Kit is neither handsome nor ugly. He has an average height, weight and build. He wears his hair short to appear more professional and succeeds only in looking slightly less interesting. I don't say any of this to be unkind. As I've already stated, Kit is one of my favourite people. He would be the first to admit all of the above.

"Kit, you're just in time. I'm being crazed and obsessive."

He followed me into another room. The former bedroom contained no furniture and I had covered one wall with photographs, photocopied notes and a web of string to connect them.

"Interesting design choices." he said.

"What do you think?"

"If you ever sell, you'll have to redecorate first."

He sat on the floor with his back against the far wall, directly across from my home-made mural. I began to talk him through it, pointing at each element as I referenced it. I hoped my enthusiastic delivery might prompt a more favourable response than the facts deserved.

"Here's what we have. You're running a play out of London. You cross paths with a group selling illegal weapons. You're onto something, so the British arrange for you to stay on. They forget to warn you that they have a guy working the same group. You talk to the smugglers for two months, hoping to meet their boss, whose name you never learn, whose face you never see. When you push them on it, the smugglers demand some time with your boss and proof of finance. I act the part because I'm in London anyway. It goes wrong, shots are fired, and undercover guy saves my life. Two days later, all the smugglers we know are dead and their boss has covered his tracks. And six months of questions later, we have this."

I pointed optimistically at the information on the wall. Kit surveyed it carefully because he wanted to spare my feelings the severity of an immediate response.

"We have nothing." he said eventually.

I looked at the complicated network of evidence I'd carefully constructed.

"... I know. I needed to hear someone else say it."

I trusted Kit's judgment. He's smart, he's loyal and we'd been through a lot. He's honest and decent and he would be a success in almost any honest, decent line of work.

Unfortunately, we both work for the CIA.

Kit dragged junk from the chairs so that we could sit down. He took the far end of the sofa. I picked an expensive, standalone chair that was designed for broken people like me. I can sit in it for an hour before my legs hurt. I only last 15 minutes in anything else.

I told Kit about the doctor's limited release on my return to work. He was polite, supportive and unconvincing in response. Reduced level would drive me crazy and he knew it.

I summarized the situation for the person who already knew it better than anyone, other than me.

"For a split second, everything was great. Then, in the space of 24 hours, they discovered I'd stalled an investigation, Leah found out about it, your cover failed and my meet went wrong. We wrecked both of our careers, estranged my leg from the rest of my body and I can't even catch the guy who called the hit. … One bad week and I'm still paying for it. We both are."

"You need to let it go."

"I don't think I can … but maybe it's time to change the angle. I may never get the guy who tried to end my life. Maybe I should thank the guy who saved it."

The American version of the attempt on my life is classified. My superiors told me that I wasn't permitted to read it and for some reason didn't understand why this would inspire me to steal a copy at the first opportunity.

Although I'd retrieved the American case file months earlier, I'd never seen the equivalent British account. I persuaded Kit to track down a copy.

Despite his professional underachievement and occasional bad luck, Kit is a clever guy, particularly with computers. Obtaining the file was possible for me, but it was child's play for him.

My reduced level and Kit's stubbornly poor track record had presented us with spare time and limited responsibility. He returned successfully less than two hours after his exit. I knew immediately he had news about Evan Noah because a closed door implied something confidential and important. Our bosses didn't trust either of us with anything confidential anymore. Many of the criticisms against us were unfair, but we still struggled to shake the consequences of our failed assignment.

"They let you take the file?" I said.

"No, I stole it, copied it and put the original back."

"Good work. What does it say?"

"They gave him a medal. He got name-checked by the academies as a role model."

"Did he make a full recovery?"

Kit didn't reply. He passed me the folder and allowed me to read the details for myself. A painful shiver left my tense neck, slid down my twisted spine and settled in my shattered knee. Noah's injuries were even worse than mine.

Kit and I weren't the only ones suffering the consequences of our failed assignment.

We decided to go for an early lunch. We walked slowly, partly as a courtesy to my reduced mobility, but also in response to our shared apathy for our afternoon's assignments. I limped more than normal due to a mysterious escalation of a dull pain that stretched from my left shin to my lower back. I'd discussed this with my doctor and he'd advised me to rest. His answer to everything was rest.

"I should have looked into this." I said.

"You had your own problems."

"Not that I could be this ungrateful."

We walked in silence for a minute and considered the hypothetical rewards we could deliver to my Good Samaritan.

"We give him money." Kit said finally.

"He saved my life."

"We give him lots of money."

"That won't work. The British would learn about it, and then Silas would know about it, and then I'd *hear* about it. We have to be more creative."

Silas Gower was our department's foremost authority on Great Britain. He had more contacts there than anyone I knew. It would be difficult for me to accomplish anything across the Atlantic without his knowledge.

"We could help Noah's career." I said.

"They already believe he's a hero. If they were going to restart his career, they'd have done it already. What else did it say in his file?"

"He's into world peace."

"We're barely speaking to most of our department. I don't think we can get him world peace."

"He'd like to date a supermodel called Ada Kala."

"If we could swing that, I'm pretty sure the Director would have set that up for himself by now."

"OK." I said. "Last thing. He supports a soccer team called Southampton. He'd like them to win the English soccer league."

Kit paused to consider the available options.

"Ada Kala's agent, do we have a phone number?"

We were invited to a presentation with 16 other people. A previous meeting from which we'd been excluded overran and kept all 16 of them occupied. Kit and I claimed the long table's far corner and whispered in the empty boardroom.

"You were over there for a while. Help me out. Explain to me again why this soccer deal is a no go."

"You've got three or four teams that could win that league." Kit explained. "Your guy's team isn't one of them."

"So, we give them some help."

"They need more than help. We're talking money, personnel and results for a nine-month window."

"We've taken corporations. We've brought down governments. How difficult could it be to interfere with a sport?"

"Nick, it's a bad idea. Think of something else."

"Unless Ada Kala is available Thursday, there is nothing else."

We brainstormed around some other options, but nothing caught our interest. Kit already knew what I was planning. He knew I don't like being told I won't win.

"You honestly think we couldn't do it?"

Kit leaned towards me and lowered his voice as if we were already co-conspirators in the scheme.

"You want to fix the results of a sport you don't play, don't watch and don't understand in a country where you're not welcome and not stationed, underneath the noses of their government, their secret service and your ex-girlfriend?"

"You're in, aren't you?"

"My mom warned me not to play with kids like you."

I've known Kit for a long time, so believe me when I tell you his insult was also his sign-on.

"What do we need?" I asked.

"A cash investment with no return, five workers at short notice, an insider on the board, some world-class players, the best sports coach in the universe and a miracle."

"Do you want to get the staff, the money or the miracle?"

"I'll take the money. Will Silas let you into Britain?"

I didn't report to Silas, but he was influential. He possessed the unquestioned and unofficial ability to approve or block transfers to the United Kingdom whenever he wished.

"Why wouldn't he?" I asked rhetorically.

I requested a meeting with Silas to discuss his denial of my request before he officially received it.

Silas Gower's office was large, but sparse and impersonal. He had no personal items or family photographs. The room intimidated some. So did Silas.

His body was frailer than I remembered, but his mind was as brilliant as ever. I respected him a lot, without actually liking him. He respected me too, but he rarely admitted this because confessing affection for a trouble-maker could be misinterpreted as affection for trouble.

"How are you?" he asked.

"I'm fine."

I wasn't fine, but an enquiry of well-being from a senior manager with full access to medical, performance and psychiatric evaluations is never a request for information.

"I saw your request. I'd like you to withdraw It and resubmit it after I've retired."

"That won't work. I'd like to visit London again and I have to consider the possibility that you might live forever."

"I think that's unlikely." he replied honestly.

Silas Gower looked like a man who'd died already and continued to sit at his desk and answer e-mails through an impressive feat of science.

"This is not a good time for you to be in London," he said. "for reasons that you are both aware of and mostly responsible for."

"I'd defend that if I didn't take so much pride in it."

"You've been to London on our behalf three times. We withdrew you the first time at the British government's request. We withdrew you the second time because the British government were about to request it. The third time, you returned for medical treatment after an attempt on your life."

"I believe that I can still make you an offer you can't refuse."

"I await it with little to no excitement."

"I'll write down two events that I will achieve in the next two months, independent of my assignment. You'll read them, approve my transfer and then burn the pieces of paper in an overly dramatic fashion."

"Very cinematic. Have you been watching many movies recently?"

"Two a day for the last six months."

"I thought so."

I scribbled down the two promises and showed them to Silas.

"I would be immeasurably grateful for number 1." he said. "Number 2 might prompt me to rewrite my will with you as a prominent beneficiary."

"I'm not in your will already?"

"No, but I owe money to some casinos and I gave them your address."

Silas leaned forward with a lighter and set the two pieces of paper alight. He dropped them into an empty coffee cup where they quickly disintegrated.

"Nick, if you repeat this conversation to anybody, I'll deny it and end your career."

"We can keep it between us. What could you open in London?"

"A training exercise out of The Old House. It's below your level."

An opportunity to corrupt the young and naïve? It was perfect.

Todd Perry is as scruffy as I am. The difference between our motives is that mine is a deliberate pattern of neglect and his is a cleverly constructed disguise. He is a millionaire, perhaps several times over, but none of this is apparent from his appearance. Somewhere below his extreme untidiness, he's probably good looking.

He spends most of his days in his office, surrounded by dismantled electrical equipment and bulky, coma-inducing manuals, doing the absolute minimum of work. The office is part of his disguise. He uses it to discourage visitors because visitors usually want his help.

Kit entered uninvited and closed the door behind him. He looked for a second chair, failed, and leaned against a nearby cabinet instead. Todd ignored him, hoping it might result in an admission of defeat and departure. It didn't work.

"Can I help you?" Todd said finally.

"Yes, I think you can."

"Sorry. Wrong answer. Trick question."

"Maybe you'll make an exception."

"If I make exceptions, people expect exceptions, and they stop being exceptions. I'm devoted to my life and my happiness. You want help or advice? They have phone lines for that."

"I'm asking on behalf of Nick Hadley."

Todd hesitated and then flicked a switch on a black box behind him that he'd clumsily labelled 'Privacy'.

"For Nick? I'll think about it." Todd said. "What does he want to do?"

"He wants to embezzle money from the CIA."

The Presidents were the new urban legend. Their story was temporarily a more popular tale than my trip to London. Some said that they were among the most gifted recruits of their graduating class. However, they had clashed with their supervisor over a hypothetical assignment that he'd argued was impossible. They'd proved him wrong by running the plan for real, including the part where they had allegedly drugged him and all of their classmates. They'd survived the inconclusive investigation, but they found themselves unclaimed by a collection of supervisors who'd heard rumours of what had happened to the previous one.

I loved them already.

I walked past a group of marksmen and reached the far end of the range. I waited patiently alongside the final shooter, Maggie Kennedy. She sensed that someone was there, but completed her perfect round before turning to face me. She hesitated as she tried to determine why she recognized me.

"Nick Hadley?"

"That's right. You might have a heard a story about me."

She smiled. She'd heard it.

"I'm looking for recruits to corrupt to my way of thinking."

"You're Operations. Why would you be on a graduate training assignment?"

"I've got health problems that slow me down. You can't save the world at my new top speed. Tell me about The Presidents."

"Jackson, Adams and Kennedy. Did you see the report?"

"I want to hear your version."

She paused. She knew I'd heard the stories about her and I was here anyway.

"The report *is* our version." she replied. "Every word is true."

"Call Adams and Jackson. As of tomorrow, you're all assigned to me."

Todd talked quickly, with an infectious enthusiasm.

"When a project is authorized, funds are set aside, sometimes up to two years in advance. You can take the money if you know where to look, how to ask and the passwords to clear it. If it's back before it's needed, no one will know it left."

"We can borrow millions if we return it within the two years?"

"Exactly. Now, they'll figure it out if you put it in your bank account but, and this is the trick, you can transfer it into a fully-authorized project. No one will know because it's an internal transfer and funding of projects is need-to-know to prevent comparisons and jealous complaints."

"How much can we get?"

"There's additional security for every zero and you never know when they'll round up. I wouldn't risk more than 499 million. How is Nick planning to spend it?"

"I shouldn't say."

"OK, but I can fix my schedule. If Nick's breaking laws and causing chaos, I want in."

I don't have much contact with either of my parents. I rarely speak to my father and I never speak to my mother.

My father is a remarkable man and a very bad father. My mother is a remarkable woman and used to be a good mother. She's a wonderful person in many ways, but it's impossible for us to interact without clashing over her obsessive hatred of her ex-husband.

He hates her for divorcing him, gaining custody of me, moving me around the country to minimize his access to me and her encouragement that I should hate him as much as she does.

She hates him for lying to her, cheating on her, continually prioritizing his work ahead of her and, in a roundabout sort of a way, my refusal to hate him as much as she does.

The turning point in my relationship with my mother was my father's assistance with my university education. Six years after their divorce, his phone calls secured a place at the college that hosted my first degree. His money cleared all the required payments, a gesture that limited my graduation debt to living expenses.

I don't condone the way he treated my mother, but he never asked me to. He made mistakes and he has to live with those, but he believed he had certain financial obligations as a parent and I agreed with him. I never felt guilty for accepting his help. My mother thought I'd forgiven him and never forgave me.

Despite my mother's belief that my acceptance of money would pull me closer to my father, it wasn't true. When I later selected a similar career, it still didn't. My mother thinks my presence in the same building as my father carries greater significance than it does. It's just a building.

I don't know my father well as a person. We've never connected or bonded. He's more senior than me. We mix in very different circles. However, I am friendly with most of his ex-wives. Since divorcing my mother, he's made a habit of dating, and occasionally marrying, women with whom he and I work. Of all his ex-wives, my favourite is Evelyn.

Not only is Evelyn intelligent and beautiful, she has an unmistakable elegance, a sense of style that reminds me of an old-style Hollywood film star. Being around her makes me feel uncouth. I don't know anybody else that can prompt me to use the word uncouth.

I called her number on my cell as I approached her apartment door. My call went unanswered and triggered her machine message.

"Hello. This is Evelyn. I'm not answering because I don't want to talk to you. Please don't leave a message."

"Hello Evelyn."

Evelyn opened her front door and I disconnected my call. I didn't ask her how she knew I was there. I glanced over her shoulder and the apartment was as stylish as I'd imagined.

She tried to hide it, but she was pleased to see me.

"I'm impressed." I said.

"I'm on holiday." she replied.

"Are you having a nice holiday?"

"Yes, I am. Thank you for asking about my holiday because you're about to ask for my help and my reply will be 'I'm on holiday'."

"It isn't work. It's a training exercise in need of a villain. I'll pay you to sleep, shop, eat, and then drop a package each Friday."

"Why me?"

"Your presence will make us look more respectable on paper and you'll keep out of projects I run alongside the main operation."

"And finally, you deliver the punch line."

"You'll do it?"

"... You had me at Hello."

Evelyn is the only person I know who can still make that line work.

Kit visited my apartment the evening before our flight. We sat in the midst of my home's escalating untidiness and reviewed our preparations. I summarized the problem and then followed up with what we had in place to secure a solution.

"Todd Perry, Evelyn Frazier, three trainees, a transfer from Silas, a 499 million dollar loan, flights booked, a reservation at The Old House and a lead for a potential insider."

"We've got everything but that miracle." Kit replied.

"We won't need one." I promised. "It's a badly organized, poorly protected, nonsense sport."

"You're confident for a man who's never watched a game of soccer from start to finish."

"It's a sport. How complicated can it be?"

In answer to my question, he reached into his pocket and pulled out a small parcel. It was wrapped in the kind of bright paper you'd expect to see on a 7 year old child's birthday present.

"We can still stop this." Kit said.

"I'm not stopping. You know that."

"I had to ask."

I nodded. We were about to start a chain of events and I had to accept responsibility for everything that resulted.

I unwrapped the parcel to reveal a children's guide to soccer. He'd bookmarked the offside rule.

What I Did When I Wasn't Saving the World (Part 2)

We walked under a sign that welcomed us to London. We were the second and third members of the team to arrive. Evelyn beat us by six hours. I don't keep track of how frequently she beats me, but if I did, I would have lost count a long time ago.

"Which car rental company did you go with?" Kit asked.

I didn't reply. I had a vague recollection of agreeing to organize our transportation, but I had no recollection of completing the task due to my not having actually completed it.

"You did organize transportation?"

"It's a work in progress." I replied.

"I got the flight, the cash, our gear and the brains. You didn't even get us a rental car?"

"It's an easily remedied situation." I said. "Evelyn taught me something I've always wanted to try. In seven seconds, look upwards and smile."

I don't remember everything I'm taught, but I make a special exception for everything I learn from Evelyn.

Simon Walker is a part-time London cab driver and a full-time agent for British intelligence. He sports a Santa-style beard and a gut he's cultivated with a dedicated beer diet. He drives a beaten-up black cab whose dents speak of his driving ability.

Two minutes after I smiled for their cameras, Walker was notified of my arrival. They knew about my arrival. They wanted me to know that they knew about my arrival. They didn't know I wanted them to know about my arrival because their predictable reaction was cheaper than a rental.

Kit and I joined the line for cabs. Walker pulled up twenty seconds later.

"Taxi for Hadley." Walker shouted.

I grinned and carried my bag towards the waiting cab. Kit asked me what had happened, but I ignored the question. Walker presented us with a sincere, Cheshire cat grin.

"Welcome to London."

I thanked him because it was a nice gesture and I was honestly delighted to be back. When you find out more about my previous visits, you might question the wisdom of this delight.

Walker dropped us at our destination, a safe house called The Old House. My employer has a large number of secret locations in the city and The Old House is the worst kept secret of these secrets.

It's a three-storey detached, surrounded by a wall and metal gates. It's almost 500 years old, but it's in good condition.

The other houses in the street are equally regal and expensive. I heard a rumour that three other countries have secret locations in the same road.

I unlocked the door and invited Kit to enter first. We heard footsteps from the top floor.

"You go ahead." I said. "I'll wait to see who's home."

Kit disappeared through a door at the back of the main foyer. Moments later, Ed Williams, a vain, intelligent twenty-something, skipped the last few steps and landed heavily on the floor beside me.

"You must be the runner." I said.

A runner is a messenger, a poorly paid intern with low responsibilities and high security clearance. They make for valuable friends and inconvenient enemies. Ed was the runner between The Old House and the embassy.

"That's me." he replied.

"How long have you been here?"

"Twelve months in London and three weeks at The Old House."

"I'm glad you're here. The embassy would fall apart without its runners."

"I'm glad you think so. Are you senior enough to sign my expenses form?"

"Not any more. I'm Nick."

I offered my hand. Ed shook it and flashed a brief, superficial smile. There was a lot to instinctively dislike about him.

"When will you be at the Embassy?" I asked.

"Later today and earlier if you need it."

"Later is fine, but accept some advice. There's a rumour that messengers don't get killed and it's not true. Plan your escape route before you mention my name to Leah Chamberlain."

The rear of The Old House's main floor is called the basement, an architecturally inaccurate description for which I've never heard an explanation. At one point in its history, perhaps when its secret location was still a secret, senior agents claimed the higher floors and lesser colleagues were consigned lower, and it's possible that basement was used as an overly dramatic label. It's a guess on my part, but I've never heard anything better.

The basement was large, open plan and badly lit. It boasted eight evenly-spaced desks, each loaded with high-tech computer equipment. Kit had claimed the desk closest to the door, the last location I would have selected. I drifted instinctively as far from the exit as I could.

I'll confess that there are parts of this story for which I wasn't present. I reserve the right to include them, in part to present key elements of the story, but also as an opportunity to portray people I don't like in a negative light. Most of these segments will involve Conrad Dean.

Conrad is a politician from a long line of politicians. I am not a fan of politicians as a general rule, although I've met both good and bad ones. Conrad epitomizes the bad. I'm not the only person to think so, which is why he has Adam Lewis, a bodyguard in all but title.

Adam Lewis is a monster of a man. He's the tallest, toughest guy in the room, in any room. I wouldn't be surprised if his presence is enough to discourage most problems before they occur. I wouldn't be surprised if his hobbies included devouring anyone who tries to cross his bridge.

The morning I arrived in London, Conrad was fielding questions regarding the latest drama to involve the government's embattled Foreign Minister. As the journalists swarmed, Adam hovered menacingly in the background. He is world class at both scowling and intimidation.

"May I ask for a comment on today's events?" the American reporter asked.

"The Foreign Secretary is a good man and he doesn't deserve the criticism he's receiving. Not a single member of the opposition would fare better than my colleague under these difficult circumstances."

"Some people say he'll be a victim of the next cabinet reshuffle and that you might one day be the man to take his position."

"I won't respond to that. The role of Foreign Minister is occupied by a gifted colleague and friend."

"Do your outspoken views on Americans make you unsuitable for foreign secretary?"

American journalists always asked him this question. Each instance was as inevitable and as infuriating as the last.

"I have already stated that the anti-American quotes attributed to me are unfounded and fictitious. I have tremendous respect for the American people."

Conrad entered his office, followed by Adam Lewis.

"I understand why they let journalists into the corridor, but why foreign journalists?"

"I think it's a law, something to do with freedom of the press."

"We also have laws about pest control. If I'm harassed every day by these people it's only a matter of time before I catch something."

"That's very global village of you."

"The Americans want to finish me. They don't want strong-willed politicians who stand up to their megalomania."

"Are you going to include that in your speech tomorrow?"

"Hating Americans is like urinating. All British politicians do it, but it's considered impolite to do so publicly. The next year is very important for me. When the Foreign Secretary loses his job due to his inexplicably limitless stupidity, the violent scramble for his position will end more political careers than a failed election campaign. Eventually, the superior candidate will be approached for the role and I will accept. The only potential banana-skin to this is Hadley. I suppose you know who that is."

Adam knew. British agents studied the tale of my ill-fated visit to their island in as much detail as the Americans.

"I won't let Hadley ruin this for me. I'm going to need your help."

"I'm your intelligence liaison. I'm not your PA."

"As long as you're assigned to me, you'll do as I say."

"As long as I'm assigned to you, I'll follow whichever orders I feel like. If you don't like that, arrange for my transfer back to real work. Remember, I'm only assigned to you because you've talked your way into death threats."

"Fine, but I still need your help. Perhaps we should look from your point of view. What do you need?"

"A rich man like you could spare small change."

"You want me to bribe you?"

"It's not bribery, it's compensation."

"What level of compensation?"

"That depends. What do you want me to do?"

I've only met Conrad Dean twice. That averages to once every two decades. You would think, in that context, there would be insufficient reason for his antagonistic feelings towards me. In his defence, our two meetings were memorable. The same two incidents also explain why two of my visits to England ended abruptly.

Our first encounter was an unfortunate clash between two young, ambitious men, both under the influence of alcohol. I was attending a function hosted by the American Embassy during a trip to London. I was distraught over a breakup with a woman whose name I honestly can't recall.

The beautifully decorated room was crowded with beautiful dressed people. I weaved around the room for half of the evening, simultaneously attempting to look busy and avoid conversation.

Conrad Dean was my social opposite. He was the heart of a crowd, wearing a self-important air and an instantly dislikeable face, neither of which he has lost in the years since. I'm not the only person to feel this way about his face.

As he reached the end of a monologue, I heard him share the following opinion.

"America is a remarkable and beautiful country, full of ignorant, arrogant, overweight people, obsessed with helping the world when they'd do better to resolve their own idiocy, obesity and lack of humility."

I carried on walking and allowed the sentence to sink in. I repeated it silently to myself as I considered his views, an exercise I credit with enabling my perfect recall of his words many years later.

I considered my response, calmly returned the length of the room and punched him in the face.

We didn't meet for another ten years because I was frequently omitted from the guest list of functions arranged by the British and Conrad was typically excluded from parties arranged by the Americans.

A decade after our first encounter, we were both included in an event planned by the Canadians, an unfortunate, understandable oversight from a nation that tries to like almost everyone. I was sober, but Conrad was drunk due to a recent by-election defeat from which his career has regrettably recovered.

He shared a new philosophy about Americans. In retaliation, I shared a theory with him about politicians. I can't remember the exact wording but it goes something like this.

If you view the political community as ministers, their aides, advisors, researchers and commentators, individuals within that community have a 62% chance of having a serious relationship within the community. 49% of those relationships produce a child, 25% of whom eventually join the same community. In summary, individuals within the community have a 74% chance of having one or more close family members within the community.

You may wonder where I obtained these statistics, at which point I would confess that I invented them. Conrad didn't know that. I continued to quote these types of figures for about two minutes and then I suggested that there were consequences to relationships within small communities and this raised genetic question marks about 5% of politicians.

Conrad is a fourth generation politician.

He couldn't get his inebriated brain around the numbers, but he knew what I was implying about the 5%. Anyway, in case I was being too subtle, I asked if he was one of them.

These two incidents, along with some poor decisions from my third business trip to London, are the reason some Americans were nervous about my return. John Rum was one of them.

John Rum, the American Ambassador to Great Britain, is a tireless, selfless individual. He's a true and loyal servant to his country. He's the living embodiment of how our diplomatic service should behave overseas. I base these comments on quotes, reports and other unreliable, politicized text. I base my opinion on quotes and reports because, despite my previous visits and three scandals of varying degrees of seriousness, I've never actually met him.

His tenure started after my second trip. During my third visit, I dealt exclusively with his personal aide, Leah Chamberlain. I can state confidentially that Leah possesses all the qualities that people attribute to her boss. She is hard-working, patriotic and no-nonsense. Somewhere below the all-business attitude, the serious tone and the semi-permanent frown are a pretty face and a beautiful smile. I know the smile is beautiful because I've seen it. I'm also the reason she frowns so much.

I slid into her office when her staff was on lunch to avoid the inefficiency of requesting an appointment. She feigned deep concentration, but instinctively knew about my arrival. She's difficult to out-smart.

From the moment our conversation started, it rattled back and forth at high speed with barely a pause between comments. If you've seen Rosalind Russell rebuke Cary Grant, you'll know what I mean.

"You can take the man out of the agency. You can't take the agency out of the man."

"The guidelines say to be as quiet as possible."

"I know." she said. "I wrote the guidelines."

"Is John in?"

She finally looked up from her paperwork.

"Not to you."

"Is he avoiding me?"

"No, but by a strange coincidence, he will always be busy when you wish to see him."

"Is he scared I'm going to cause an international incident?"

"Everyone who's ever met you is scared you'll cause an international incident. When you inevitably invite disaster on yourself and those around you, he'd prefer to plead ignorance than apologize for even the smallest involvement."

"I'm here for two months."

"He has a lot of meetings."

"Whose people do I liaise with?"

"Mine."

"Why yours?"

"Life hates me."

"Does Rum know our history?"

"I explained my complicated feelings for you, but his decision was final."

"You still talk faster than anyone I know."

"The faster I talk, the sooner the conversation ends."

"When can I see you?"

"I hope you mean professionally."

"I hope I don't."

"Be serious for a second."

"I can offer a serious second. I struggle with entire minutes."

"I expect weekly reports."

"I won't deal through junior staff. If I can't see John Rum, I'll deal with you, and I'm not meeting here because the meetings are pointless, I'll be busy, and I'll want to combine the reviews with lunch."

"The meetings are not pointless. The embassy needs to know what you're doing before you do it."

"The meetings *are* pointless because I won't tell you anything worth knowing. They're just the precautionary phase of the inevitable blame storming you'll set up to deflect my mistakes away from yourselves. Do you want an initial appraisal or should we set up for next week?"

"We want an initial appraisal. We need to prepare to deflect your mistakes away from ourselves."

"Tomorrow lunchtime. I'll let you know where."

"You never said sorry."

I racked my brain unsuccessfully for a memory that would prove her wrong. I should have and I would have, but my accident and my injury had sent me stateside and stolen my chance.

"I was going to. I got ... distracted."

"You're not distracted now."

"I'm sorry."

Leah smiled weakly. She'd deserved an apology. I was six months late.

When Kit and I had discussed our plans, we'd agreed that we needed an insider, somebody we could insert into the company in question. It had to be someone who would tolerate our plans. It had to be someone that the company would accept as plausible. It had to be someone with enough money that our contribution wouldn't raise questions. We completed our search before leaving America and found our perfect candidate. The only complication was that our insider didn't know this yet.

William McRae was a billionaire businessman on his third career after growing bored of success in his first two. His new challenge was the European division of an American-owned multi-national with close financial ties to the CIA. It was this connection, along with a happy coincidence, that had secured his position as our favourite candidate.

I arrived unannounced at the divisional headquarters on the south coast of England. I flirted with the building's receptionist and provided the kind of impressive, fraudulent biography that would secure me 30 seconds with a man of McRae's importance.

I sat in their lobby reading a company brochure while I waited. I selected a comfortable chair that didn't trouble my legs and lower back as much as most. I recognised McRae the moment he entered the room. He had a confidence and a presence that was immediately impressive. He looked younger than his 60 years.

"Nick, good to meet you. I'm William McRae."

I placed the brochure back on the table and followed McRae down the corridor.

"How are things in New York?" he asked.

"I honestly wouldn't know."

He stopped abruptly and turned to face me.

"I was told you were from our head office."

"I may have exaggerated."

"Mr. Hadley, I am a very busy man. I found time for you because I was led to believe you were from our parent company."

"No, Mr. McRae, I'm from the company that owns your parent company."

"... I don't know what you mean."

"Yes, you do. Make some calls."

McRae welcomed me into his office. He was polite, but suspicious.

"Mr. Hadley. Please sit down."

I selected the seat opposite McRae.

"I've been able to confirm your identity," he said. "but not the reason for your visit."

"I'd like to transfer some money from one of our accounts. I can provide paperwork that suggests you obtained the funds from aggressive and successful share dealing. Then I'd like you to invest this money in a British company and join the board of directors where you'll influence policy, both on a financial and practical level. I believe that this investment, and your respected business knowledge, would be of value to the company in question."

"How much?"

I wrote the number on a piece of paper and showed it to him.

"That's a lot of money." he said.

"Yes, it is."

"What's the name of the company?"

I wrote the name of Evan Noah's favourite soccer team on the same piece of paper.

"Is this a joke?"

"I can't go into details, but we have reasons for wishing this company some level of success."

"Are you aware that although I have had no direct financial involvement, I've taken an interest in this company's ... field activities for forty years?"

I knew. It was why we'd selected him.

McRae looked around the room and completed a slow, steady breath.

"I'm ... I'm stunned. This is genuinely a dream come true. If I rubbed a lamp without realizing, do I get two more wishes?"

I smiled. We had our insider.

"Yes, you get two more wishes. And if you'll allow me to make a suggestion, ask for a league title and a cup final. I'll see what I can do."

Later that afternoon, I had my first update meeting with Leah. I picked the location and selected a romantic Italian restaurant. She didn't approve of my choice. From the moment she entered, she looked ready for a fight.

She noticed a violinist performing a series of slow melodies and approached the head waiter instead. She subtly slipped him some money.

"Tell the violinist that if he comes near my table, I will damage something precious to him. I don't mean the violin."

The waiter nodded and took a step backwards.

Leah took the only other chair at our two person table. She stared at me angrily.

"What?" I said. "I like Italian food."

"I'm not staying to eat. Let's be quick about this."

"It's a basic training op; three trainees looking for evidence of bad behaviour. Kit is running the team. I'm in dual roles as bad guy and assistant coach. Evelyn Frazier is in London to receive the drops."

"Evelyn Frazier? I'm surprised. I thought you only worked with reprobates. I was initially concerned about your influence on the trainees until I saw their files. Did you hear what they did to their classmates?"

"I smile about it to this day."

"I don't want them at the embassy."

"I'll keep them at The Old House. I met the runner, Ed Williams. Is he any good?"

"He's fast enough, but he's ambitious. Be careful."

"Thanks. I'll keep that in mind."

"Do you want to tell me about Todd Perry? What is your official lie for his involvement?"

"I want someone clever at The Old House to pass on knowledge. Todd is good with computers and he's the best there is with finance."

"I don't want him at the embassy either. We won't be a source."

"I don't know what you mean."

"Yes, you do. Are we finished?"

"No. I want you to see this."

I passed her a copy of a case file, the one they'd tried to keep from me by reminding me that I wasn't supposed to read it.

"How did you get this?"

"Does it matter?"

She flicked to the bookmarked pages and read the paragraphs I'd highlighted. Leah's expression faded from anger to concentration.

"It says here you exonerated Kit from blame and they ignored you."

"I know you're concerned about the trouble I may cause, but if this training exercise attracts any controversy, they'll end Kit's career. I won't let that happen. Satisfied?"

She handed back the file.

"... I've got to go. I'll call in a few days."

I nodded and Leah walked for the exit. The waiter completed a precautionary retreat before she passed him.

Erich Maier may be the best soccer coach in the world. The jury is out on that one, but it says a lot that he's part of the discussion. William McRae thinks he is and that's good enough for me.

Erich Maier was temporarily out of work because of allegations that he might be a crook. The jury is out on that one too.

McRae, the new part owner of an English soccer team, arranged to meet him at an airport, not far from Maier's home. McRae flew in first class and I travelled in the cheap seats of the same plane. McRae met Maier at an airport restaurant and I kept line of sight from a nearby bar.

"As I was saying, I have invested heavily in this club. I want success in return for that investment. I think you can bring the kind of success I'm after and I'd like to discuss the possibility of you becoming their manager."

Maier replied in broken, heavily-accented English.

"I am honoured that you would think of me."

McRae scratched at the side of his head. He wasn't used to the small earpiece I'd inserted in his right ear. I carefully listened to the conversation and fed it when necessary.

"Everyone I have spoken to agrees that if we are going to be as great as I believe we can, we need your help."

As Maier considered the offer, I plotted my next line. My instincts told me that we were 30 seconds from hiring our world class coach. We were about to obtain another piece of our puzzle.

"I thank you for your offer. I cannot accept. As you know, I am under investigation by the sport's governing bodies. They're bringing charges against me and I may not be able to work in football for several years."

I let his statement hang for a few seconds and then prompted McRae's next line.

"Ask him how grateful he'll be if you make the criminal charges go away."

An hour before my return to London, Todd Perry landed at Gatwick. An hour after I arrived, The Presidents landed at Heathrow.

As I entered the basement, I spotted Todd in the shadows of the far corner. He'd moved my minimal possessions to a nearby seat and claimed the farthest desk from the door for himself. He looked weary and antisocial. He appeared to be actively avoiding any source of light.

"Todd, good to see you. How was the flight?"

"Psycho pilot. I think he faked turbulence for a joke."

"Yes, I heard they teach that at flight schools. Will you be OK?"

"I'll hack the airline's head office later. That's usually good for a few more days of sanity. I hear you've been to Germany. See the sights?"

"Two planes and an airport."

"That sounds about right."

I sat down beside him.

"Todd, we're making this up as we go along. You think outside the box even more than I do. If you have ideas, I want to hear them."

"I'm going to like working for you, aren't I?"

"Yeah, you are. Any other questions?"

"I heard you're unpopular in Britain."

"I heard that too."

"How does that affect me?"

"This is an authorized training assignment. They'll suspect I'm running private schemes, but they've no reason to suspect your involvement."

"In other words, the people who curse your very existence have no interest in me at all."

"No offence intended."

Todd smiled. No offence taken.

But I would be followed. As a consequence, I would have to keep out of as much of the operational work as possible. I would offer whatever support I could from this room. The rest of the time, I'd be playing hide and seek with British intelligence.

Kit appeared in the doorway.

"Nick. They're here."

Three people followed him into the room. The first was Maggie Kennedy. Thanks to memorization of their files, I recognised the two men behind her as Dan Jackson and Ben Adams. Dan and Ben were as tall and good-looking as Maggie was short and pretty.

Dan was blond and carried a build that made me feel puny by comparison. He looked Scandinavian. All he needed was a longboat and 30 friends and he could have terrorized Northern Europe.

Ben was dark-haired and equally handsome. He reminded me of a guy from my university classes who slept with all the best looking girls.

Maggie, Dan and Ben each selected an available desk. Todd Perry glanced briefly at Maggie and then returned, jet-lagged and semi-conscious, to his screen. Kit closed the door to the foyer and then returned his attention to me.

All eyes looked in my direction. I stood slowly, leaned on a nearby wall for support and delivered my opening pitch.

"I know you're tired. I'll keep this simple. You know why you're here. At first glance, the assignment is a joke. You're not at risk from danger or arrest or injury. This is not the kind of work that you trained for. … This assignment is for you to show me that you are ready for assignments where you risk danger and arrest and injury. If you help me with this, I will help you get your careers back on track to where they deserve to be.

"And if you need more incentive for treating this assignment seriously, believe the following. In the British government, eleven ministers list soccer as a primary interest. In the British intelligence community, nine of the ten most senior department heads follow a soccer team. This is a sport followed by tens of millions of British people and hundreds of millions worldwide. If the British learn why we're here, this will sour Anglo-American relations for decades. We need to do this secretly and successfully. We've got seven weeks."

That evening, a computer hacker working for MI5 tried to break into our system as a favour to Adam Lewis. After three hours, he admitted defeat.

The next morning, Scott Walker took his first shift as part of a rotating fleet of taxis watching The Old House. He split his attention between my base of operations and a tabloid newspaper. He read the sport news on the back pages first. Many of his countrymen do the same.

Kit Jordan, Todd Perry and The Presidents stayed in a nearby hotel, but returned by seven the following morning. I slept in a small office in the basement of The Old House. I didn't sleep well, but I never do.

Most of the team looked better than the day before with the exception of Todd who looked worse. He entered nursing a large cup of coffee. He didn't bounce back from tough days until his morning caffeine permitted it.

Kit passed each of them some hand-outs and I issued their first instructions.

"The mission starts here. Each week, we'll meet together, we'll brainstorm and we'll authorize or reject each suggestion. All ideas are welcome. No rejections are personal. All high tech goes through Kit. All finance goes through Todd. I've assigned each of you a soccer team that stands between us and what we want to achieve. I want you to research your target like you would an enemy cell. You need to know them better than they know themselves. This weekly meeting and the ones that follow are where you bring your ideas for how to ensure their failure. Any questions so far?"

"You've given every team a code." Dan said.

"We want to limit what people hear, but we can't guarantee total privacy at all times. From this point forward, I don't want anyone using the real names of our company or their rivals outside of this room. At my request, our insider has created coded references for all of the affected organizations. These references are names to enable easy integration into conversation. I wouldn't be surprised if he's used former personnel as inspiration."

"Is it text book to use people's names as code for key terms?"

"No, I saw it in a Nic Cage movie."

I heard Todd laugh, which suggested the caffeine was finally working.

"Let me end with this. If we succeed, no one will ever know what we achieved." I told the room. "If we fail, the whole world will know. ... Let's not fail."

Following that morning's meeting, my team knew the extent and the importance of our low profile. We all forgot to mention this to William McRae.

Ed Williams, the Old House's runner, smuggled me out the house in his car. He dropped me at a subway station and I smuggled myself into Evelyn's apartment building. I exchanged pleasantries with Evelyn and we talked about my father's professional brilliance and personal missteps. It's our go-to topic.

Evelyn responded to a polite knock and opened the door for McRae. He looked anxious and preoccupied. She invited him in and then paused, ready to make herself scarce. McRae stood near to the dinner table I had sat behind.

"Mr. McRae, we shouldn't be meeting. What do you want?"

"I couldn't sleep. I wondered if I could help."

"Haven't you got a business to run?"

"You can't put me in this position and then complain that I'm in it." he said. "I know more about football than you. I know more about this country than you. I know more about the company you just purchased than every American put together."

Evelyn shrugged her shoulders and left the room.

"You should probably sit down." I said.

As he joined me, McRae placed his briefcase on the table and opened it up. He lifted out some documents and I watched the stack of materials grow alongside it.

"I wrote down some thoughts." he said. "These are the reasons the top four teams are the top four teams. These are the five positions that we need to fill to get closer to those top four teams. These are the names of the most influential people in the game including players, coaches, chairmen, administrators, agents and referees. These are random thoughts I had, concerns that you have to address. And finally … Where is it? I know I have it somewhere. … These are the reasons we won't succeed."

I picked up this final document first.

"I can see you've been thinking about this."

"You don't appreciate how much of a knowledge resource I could be to you." McRae told me. "So, the question is, what do *you* want?"

Despite the fact that I lived, worked and slept in the same building, I was the last to arrive in our main office the following day. My body made the same complaints it made every morning, but my brain was still focused on McRae's prediction of failure. My doubts had plagued my attempts to rest in every moment my body hadn't already stolen.

In the absence of the focus I would have provided, the early discussion drifted. Todd glanced at Maggie when he thought she might not notice and failed. Maggie smiled, but said nothing. Todd, slightly embarrassed, quickly sparked a conversation to cover for his carelessness.

"Have you guys got specialties?"

Maggie pointed at herself and then Ben and then Dan.

"Weapons, Science, Communications." Maggie replied.

"Weapons?"

"Never upset her." Dan suggested. "That's all I'm saying."

I entered, carrying McRae's briefcase. I placed it on Jackson's desk and started to pull out McRae's notes.

"I've been told I'm going to fail. I'm a bad loser. I want a damage assessment and ideas for limitation, starting now. Where are we with the hacks into the competition?"

"We've got them." Kit replied.

"Which ones?"

"All of them. I'll have daily feedback from this afternoon."

"Excellent work. Maggie, Dan, Ben, you have your targets. Accelerate your research into Frank, Bryan and Niall. I want high quality recommendations on how best to ruin their lives. Todd, my day started badly. Pick a target and do something creative and mischievous."

He agreed immediately. Mischievous is his speciality.

Leah requested an update for reasons she didn't share. I took Todd with me because it was a busy day and I thought his presence might reduce the length of the meeting. We took a cab to a wine bar and Simon Walker tailed us the entire way.

I bought Todd a drink as a thank you for volunteering involvement in my ridiculous scheme prior to receiving an invitation. I let him finish his glass before I shared the news.

"I spoke with the ambassador's aide. She told me to mention some embassy rules."

"I'm banned from the embassy." he guessed.

"You're not surprised."

"They think I'll scam them for information for my share dealing, and I would too. Don't worry about it. I'm banned from every government building except for the ones I work in."

He used his honest reply as the springboard for a question of his own.

"As we're sharing secrets here," he said. "do you want to tell me the deal with you and the ambassador's secretary? Every time you mention her name, there's an edge to your voice. It's like you like her but you killed her cat and she liked the cat and she knows it was you who killed it."

"We have a love-hate relationship."

"I can guess who's got the hate part. You two have a history?"

"We dated briefly and then split up under difficult circumstances. … I may have inadvertently let people believe she was selling embassy secrets."

He didn't respond at first. It's difficult to surprise Todd, but I'd achieved it.

"Wow. I guessed the first part, but … Wow. That is not what I expected you to say."

"Todd, Leah's not John's secretary, she's his personal aide. When he's ill, she does his job. When he's well, she only does most of his job. She has a higher security clearance than us. She has friends more powerful than us. My advice? Be nice."

"Thanks for the warning. … Really? Embassy secrets?"

I didn't want to answer the question. However, I knew that if I could track down the case file, so could Todd. If I forced him to search for it, he'd complete this at the expense of the tasks I assigned him. Reluctantly providing the information he'd requested was more efficient than daring him to find it himself.

"… There was a series of leaks coming out of the London embassy. None of it was classified, but it's embarrassing when everyone knows your business. I was sent here to investigate Leah. I got to know her, I started to like her and I wanted to spend more time with her. I knew that if I cleared her, I'd be recalled. So, I … continued to investigate."

"You *stalled a mole inquiry*?" Todd whispered in a tone that suggested I had strayed into a small sub-category of stunts even he wouldn't attempt.

"It's a compliment, from a certain point of view."

"I am never asking you for advice on women. ... And she just walked in."

I turned to see Leah standing in the doorway. Todd made his excuses.

"I'll be in the … er … Yeah."

Leah took Todd's vacant seat and our adversarial conversation started immediately.

"Leah, good to see you."

"Good to see you too."

"Do you mean that?"

"No, I'm lying."

"I hope you approve of the setting. I wanted to meet somewhere with fewer stringed instruments. I didn't want to place more innocent musicians at risk."

"No, you brought Todd Perry instead and found a whole new way to upset me. I don't want him near the embassy and *I don't want him near me*. Don't bring him to our meetings."

"It won't happen again."

A server approached us and Leah scared her away with a glance before she could speak. Leah waited until she'd departed and then restarted her tirade.

"Nick, it's important that we're open about certain matters. Professionally, you can rely on me. I work harder than anyone at that embassy."

"I believe you."

"Secondly, if part of your return to London is an attempt to win me back, I'm going to make you wish we'd never met. I hope my honesty is not inappropriate."

"If we're going to work together, you can't be angry with me."

"That won't be a problem. My consuming, passionate hatred of you was replaced by a calm, rational mistrust some time ago."

"Is that because I was shot?"

"As I recall, I wanted you to suffer pain and disgrace. You unexpectedly did and that satisfied my wishes."

I tried to analyse the conflicting messages of her admission. I couldn't decide if her opinion of me was better or worse than I'd assumed.

Adam Lewis wore jeans and a T-shirt. In spite of this, he still looked like he might be a policeman. The thug wore tattoos, piercings and scars, with too many of each to count.

They met in a dark alleyway because neither wanted to be seen with the other. It would be bad for their respective credibility.

"What's the deal?" the thug asked.

He spoke in an exaggerated Cockney accent that may or may not have been genuine.

"He's American. We want him to feel unwelcome."

"Say no more. I hate Americans."

Adam handed him an envelope. The thug didn't count it. They'd worked together before.

Kit, Todd and The Presidents pulled their chairs into a circle without prompting. I joined them. I wanted to hear their ideas. Despite what we'd already set in motion, every Monday morning was crucial.

"Let's take a look at Niall. He's going to be a key rival."

"I want to set up a gradual leak of half-truths and lies through the Internet." Dan replied. "I think we can send out messages that will turn the staff against each other, get them too busy arguing to kick-start a challenge.

"Every sports team has egos and tantrums. How much will in-fighting make a difference?"

"It'll work."

"You make it sound like you've pulled this trick before."

"I'm the youngest of six brothers. I pulled this trick every day for eighteen years."

"OK. Make it happen. Maggie, we know Bryan will be a problem."

"They're the favourites because of some rumoured signings, but they may play into our hands. They have four high profile players moving on and another three retiring. If we let the players move on and then block the players coming in, they'll have a staff shortage."

"And we can mess with incoming signings for more than just Bryan." Todd interrupted. "Some of the clubs rely on the money they get from the TV companies. I can engineer a contract delay with that agreement. If TV pays up in eight months instead of eight weeks, that'll disrupt a lot of plans."

"But some of these clubs are owned by millionaires."

"I'm confident I can distract them away from soccer for a six month window."

"And the clubs owned by shareholders?"

"I'm going to temporarily collapse the market for shares in British sporting teams. Nobody smarter than an amoeba will leave money in these clubs."

"Can you do that?" Kit asked.

"If I showed you how easy it was, you'd never buy shares again."

"Maggie, you mentioned high profile signings." I asked. "Which of them would Bryan consider the most important?"

"If I told you his full name we'd be here another hour, but the back of his shirt reads Garcia. He's the new Batistuta."

"And Batistuta is?"

"I didn't get that far, but I'm guessing being the new one is a good thing. I want to raise doubts about Garcia's passport. He's Argentinean, but he's planning to play in Europe on a Spanish passport. There have been some passport scandals in the past. If we raise enough doubts in the newspapers, we can push him in the direction of Spain. The papers will go for it because they don't need encouragement to kick an Argentinean."

"Falklands?"

"No, they've more or less let that go, but an Argentinean scored a goal with his hand at a World Cup and English soccer fans will never forgive them."

I pulled Ben to one side after the morning meeting. He was more introverted than I had expected. I'd assumed that he would be more like Maggie and Dan, both of whom were as confident as I had assumed. He'd introduced an idea based around flu viruses and dropped it at the first opposition. I'd waited for him to reintroduce an improved version of his plan and ended the meeting disappointed.

I suspected he was the smartest of The Presidents. I suspected his confidence was at its strongest when it was just the three of them. I needed him to be that confident when it was the two of us.

"I read about your work with tranquillizing chemicals." I said.

"My background is science, specifically chemistry, so I fell back onto that for some of my assignments."

Ben had designed a mixture that, when released into the air, would cause dizziness, tiredness and nausea.

"And you tested it on your fellow trainees without warning them." I said.

"I ... don't believe that was ever conclusively proven."

"Don't worry. I'm your biggest fan. I'd like to know what would happen with a greater degree of dilution."

"Certainly not dizziness or nausea. It might affect reaction times. Depending on the length of exposure, the effects would last, maybe, twenty minutes. It would be easy to get into the air, near impossible to detect."

I passed him some documents, a collection of schematics and drawings that his analytical brain could interpret effortlessly.

"These are blueprints of the room where our client's rivals make their final preparations prior to meetings in our building. I want three proposals for how to get your magic formula into the air in *that room* every other Saturday for the next year."

He pitched his solution two hours later.

Some people like to be the smartest person in the room. Every time I entered that basement with Ben, Dan and Todd, I wasn't in the top three.

It was wonderful.

I sent Kit to see John Rum. I knew Kit would fail, but the embassy expected us to try at least once a week. It would be suspicious if we didn't humour their suspicions.

"He's in a meeting." Leah said before Kit asked.

"He can't dodge us forever."

"He can today. The meeting's in Brussels. Why do you need to see him?"

"I don't, but Silas expects us to try."

Leah nodded. She appreciated his honesty.

"Can I ask you something?" she said. "Why are you so nice to me?"

"Nick told me you have powerful friends. Actually, I think he tells everyone you have powerful friends."

She hesitated and considered how to abuse this knowledge.

"... Tell him to tell people I like chocolate."

The first three weeks of experiments and trial runs passed in a blur. We didn't sleep as much as we should have, and adrenaline and enthusiasm powered some initial success. The hacks into the rival teams fed us a regular stream of truths and half-truths that we gleefully fed anonymously to new journalistic contacts. We advertised disagreements and promoted their escalation. When we didn't find disagreements, we invented some.

In a nod to the training we were supposed to be providing The Presidents, we ran a drop at the end of each week for them to monitor, track and report. In the third of these exams, I left The Old House for the first time in several days with a small package. The Presidents tailed me, as did Simon Walker. Despite my slow speed, they all missed the drop.

People always underestimate me. It was always true, but now more than ever. They see my limp, they read the persistent pain in my expression, and they forget that I'm good at this. I'm really good at this.

Evelyn is even better. None of them saw her collect the parcel. I didn't see her either.

We met on the Monday morning to plan our next round of interference.

"His name is Pavel Hasek." Maggie said. "He's a defender, he's very talented and unofficial deals were made over a year ago."

"How do we block it?"

"I don't know. I've checked everything and I'm running out of ideas."

The room feel quiet until Todd provided an option.

"... Has he ever been injured?"

"Yes. He had a knee injury two years ago."

"Kick-start the message boards with discussions of Hasek's fitness and open-ended questions about why the other top clubs aren't chasing his signature. Add specific rumours by the end of the week alleging a serious knee injury that could only be confirmed by the kind of invasive surgery no healthy soccer player would agree to."

"What if that doesn't work?"

The room fell quiet until Todd offered the answer we were all considering.

"Then we think of a way to hurt his leg again."

Every idea we suggested enhanced our confidence. Every scheme we set in motion boosted our belief of eventual victory. Unfortunately, we all forgot to mention this optimism to McRae.

Ed Williams smuggled me out the house again. I smuggled myself into Evelyn's apartment five minutes before our insider's arrival. Evelyn responded to a polite knock and then made herself scarce.

"Mr. McRae, believe it's not a turn of phrase; we have to stop meeting like this."

"We've had a setback." he explained.

"What's the problem?"

"We've been approaching our short list of personnel for the past week and nobody is interested."

"I thought if we got Maier, we'd attract players."

"It's not happening and I think I understand why. There are two levels of competition. There are the contests that you enter in your own country and there are competitions that you enter in Europe. Only the top teams from each country are permitted to enter the European competitions and that is why we can't attract the players we've targeted. They want to play in Europe and we're not in Europe."

"There must be some way we can persuade them."

"We can't convince them of what we hope to achieve without admitting how we hope to achieve it. I don't think you're ready to tell a group of sportsman that we're rigging their national game."

"No, they can never know. We've got to think of something else."

I returned to The Old House. I waved politely to Simon Walker. He appeared irritated that he was witnessing my return after missing my departure. It wasn't the first time.

Kit was absent from the basement and I recalled giving him permission to pursue a lead that he had neglected to reveal. In the absence of my usual confidante, I hoped Todd might restore my faith, but he looked more agitated than I was. Our setbacks were arriving as if they've conspired and coordinated their arrival times.

"You need to see this."

He pulled me over to the darkest part of the room and handed me an obscured image. It looked like an official team photograph, but there was sufficient scowls and background activity that it had to be one that they'd rejected before selecting another picture from the same session.

"One of the best teams in Italy." Todd said.

I scanned the two rows of men in a team's uniform, the front row crouching on one knee so that the back row weren't obscured. They were all athletic. Their facial appearances ranged from handsome to troll-like ugliness. A caption below listed names, some of which I recognized and some of which I didn't.

"They're a soccer team." I said. "I don't get it."

"Check the background." Todd instructed.

I looked closer, this time ignoring the players and inspecting the figures behind, people caught in the photograph by accident.

"That's impossible." I said as soon as I saw him.

"I know, but it's him."

"It can't be him."

"I know, but it's him. … What do we do?"

In our line of work, it's a bad idea to learn a secret you're not supposed to know.

"I could … I could …."

I stopped talking when I realized that I had no second half to the sentence and the repetition of the first half portrayed me as indecisive and clueless, both of which were momentarily accurate.

"I could make a phone call." I said finally.

Todd accepted this as an acceptable next step. I didn't mention that I had no idea who I was calling.

My half-brother Asher and I work for the same company, albeit in different departments and on very different career paths. I'm climbing the ladder rapidly and occasionally slipping a rung. He is ascending it steadily. I travel the world on different assignments and no two projects are ever the same. He's efficiently pushed the same paperwork for years.

Asher works in Supplies and ensures that agents in all parts of the world receive the basic materials they need. He's kind of like Q from the Bond movies, if Q's focus was less on gadgets and more on office equipment.

If my tone appears condescending, that isn't my intent. I don't mean to diminish his role in any way. I like chairs and tables. I use pens daily. He is in many regards a valuable servant of our country and an unsung hero, but I struggle to relate to his contribution because I can't imagine completing such tasks myself. I could never work in a job whose moments I could predict accurately before each day commenced.

It suits Asher though. He's meticulous, methodical, organized. Routine tasks don't bother him. Paperwork doesn't smother him. He's very good at what he does. We're roughly the same grade, but he'll probably obtain his next promotion soon.

It took longer than it should have for me to consider my brother as a source of information regarding the agent in Italy. Asher is usually the first person I think of when I need to locate colleagues because Asher probably sent them stationary.

"Is this a secure line?" he asked.

"Semi-secure." I replied.

"What does that even mean?"

"I think it's secure, but there are some security protocols I haven't run."

"Which ones?"

"All of them."

"Let's talk like it's secure and it's on you if it isn't. How can I help?"

"I need to ask a question about someone." I said. "I don't want to use his name."

"That might make it more difficult for me to respond."

"He's an uncontrollable psychotic who appears in the nightmares of anyone who's ever met him."

"Oh, yeah, I know who you mean."

"Is he currently stationed in Southern Europe?"

"Yeah. Yeah, I think he is?"

"You're sure."

"I heard an audible sigh of relief from everyone based outside of Southern Europe. I think he moved about three years ago. Can I ask why you're asking?'

"You could, but don't."

"Have you crossed his path?"

"Not yet. I might."

"It was nice knowing you."

My brother's automatic association of crossing the gentleman's path and then dying as a result was an overly dramatic, cynical conclusion. I'd already reached the same conclusion.

Kit returned a day later than he had promised. It wasn't fair to blame our recent bad luck on his unexplained absence, but his failure to explain it made him an easy target. I forgave him when he shared his explanation.

He wanted to talk to me alone and waited until The Presidents were elsewhere. Todd was slumped so low in his chair that it was easy to forget his existence and he worked so many hours that it was impractical to wait for his absence.

"Being back restarted my curiosity." Kit confessed in a quiet voice. "I made a few enquiries about the night you were shot."

"Anything?"

"I don't think so. All we know about the guy who called in the hit is that he's from the south-east of England, he's a big soccer fan and he was stuck in traffic travelling from the game to your meeting. There were two matches that night and Chelsea / Arsenal was the only game in London. I checked out corporate box owners and season ticket holders. Nothing."

"There was no harm in trying."

I didn't tell him that I'd run the same checks a week earlier. I'd achieved the same disappointing results.

Todd sat up suddenly. It was impossible to tell from his expression if he was excited or terrified.

"I got the confirmation. He's a part owner in the club."

Kit didn't know the story behind the comment and he didn't know about the photograph. He wisely held his tongue.

"Does this mean what I think it means?" I said.

Todd nodded.

"We're not the first people to buy a soccer club with money from the CIA."

Dan returned with his colleagues two hours later. Their smiles were the injection of confidence I'd needed all week.

"We got them." he said.

"Who?"

"Maier called in favours from a couple of top coaches and they're going to loan us players. They're only eighteen, but they're future superstars and we've got them for the year."

"The theory goes that the youngsters will work with Maier for a year and go back to their clubs as better players." Maggie explained.

Todd joined us in the middle of the room.

"I've got you two more." he said.

He passed me an e-mail from a psychotic American based in Italy. He'd invested heavily in a soccer club and he was unhappy we knew about it. The e-mail explained that he hadn't ruled out hurting us. The message's final paragraph was an offer to loan us two players for the year in return for our silence.

I read the names of the players, players so good that they represented their countries, players so good that even I recognised their names. Without providing context to the rest of the room, I spontaneously cheered.

McRae was desperate to help us in addition to the unsolicited assistance he had already provided. We brainstormed as a team to determine how to best use his expertise. We wanted to utilize his knowledge. We wanted him to stop asking.

Kit met him at Evelyn's apartment. Evelyn disappeared into another room, true to her promise that she would keep out of my other dealings.

Kit shook McRae's hand as he entered the room. They sat at the table and Kit laid out a complex list.

"I've got a calendar and a schedule of games for you." Kit said.

"I thought they were randomly generating the fixture list on Monday."

"Yes, this is the list that they'll randomly generate. I want you to take a look and make some suggestions."

McRae scanned the document.

"Some of the teams have extra midweek games because they'll be playing in Europe. We should schedule our meetings with them immediately prior to those midweek games. We'll have a better chance against them when they're resting players."

McRae had attempted on several occasions to question me for my motives unsuccessfully. He took the opportunity to ask Kit for the same information.

"I still don't begin to understand this. Why would they trust you with so much money? Almost everyone who invests in football does so for love and not for profit. Why would they agree to this?"

Kit recalled my retelling of McRae's recruitment and replied with the same metaphor.

"I'm sorry. We gave you three wishes and you used them. If you want answers, you'll need another genie."

A very long time ago, I was kidnapped by an ex-girlfriend's ex-boyfriend.

He didn't resent me because she'd left me to return to him, which to my mind presented a strong case for my resenting him. He was upset with me because she had developed the unfortunate habit of comparing us.

She criticized the presents he bought her as inferior to mine. She told him that his time keeping was inferior to mine. She complained that his complaints about her complaints were stronger than mine would have been. She compared us with such ubiquity and ferocity that it raises serious questions as to why she'd broken up with the person who remains the individual most like me in the whole world, by which I mean me.

Unable to tolerate the constant barrage of negative feedback, he decided to gain his revenge by causing me serious physical damage. By this point in the story, you may not be shocked by his selection of strategy.

He forced me at gunpoint into the trunk of his car and drove to a secluded location. It was an uncomfortable journey because, in keeping with the crime's spontaneous nature, he'd neglected to empty the trunk first.

I'll never know how badly he would have hurt me because he forgot to confiscate my phone. I made several calls to the police and I was rescued three seconds after he opened the trunk. To this day, he's still confused as to why six police cars and a helicopter descended on such an isolated setting.

It's because of this experience that I'm open minded about travelling in the trunks of cars, particularly shorter journeys for which I have the opportunity to empty the trunk's contents beforehand. However, it can be still be an uncomfortable experience if your driver traverses streets like he's being chased by the KGB, which apparently Ed Williams does.

I didn't leave The Old House very often. When I did, Ed Williams was invaluable. I spent some of these journeys contemplating a thank you present. My first choice was driving lessons.

As was my habit, I asked him to drop me near my required location, but I neglected to tell him my intended destination or business. Today was a Friday. My business was a training exercise and a drop, or lunch with my father's ex-wife, depending on your point of view.

I arrived at the restaurant before her and scanned the streets for her approach. As if from nowhere, she appeared beside me. To this day, I don't know how she did it.

"You're late." she said.

"London traffic. What can I say?"

"You can tell me you're sorry and then buy me lunch."

She files expenses. I buy all her lunches. I humoured her request anyway.

"I'm sorry. Can I buy you lunch?"

"Yes, you may. Any news?"

"Nothing to report. Keep up the hard work."

"I've been sleeping and shopping."

"I'm sure you do both expertly."

"I like working for you."

I placed a package in her hands. Another training exercise was over. We'd completed another drop without The Presidents obtaining a single sighting of Evelyn. The previous exercises had relied on Evelyn's considerable skill. This week's failure had probably resulted from Ed William's manic driving. They would only have two more attempts. I predicted two more victories for Evelyn.

If I walk too much, my leg hurts. If I sit for too long, my leg hurts. The pain caused by these two scenarios is slightly different. After several weeks of life in a basement, and the resultant aches this had generated, I decided to shift the discomfort to a different part of my anatomy. I attempted to walk to The Old House.

I'm not sure who spotted me first. I experienced a sixth sense that suggested a tail, but when I tried to determine an American president or a British agent, I saw evidence of both.

I phoned Dan and warned him of the British presence. At my request, Dan started to follow the agent who was following me. When I lost him a few minutes later and the defeated agent switched his attention to lunch, Dan provided me with the name of the restaurant.

I arrived at his table unannounced and introduced myself. If he was surprised to see me, he didn't show it.

"Hi. I'm Nick Hadley."

"Adam Lewis." he replied.

"I've got a great idea." I said. "You tell me why you're following me and I'll tell you what I'm doing today. It will save you the trouble of following at a distance."

"If you know my current assignment, you know why I'm following you."

"Tell Conrad that I'm coaching trainees and that's all. Any requests he has that would aid Anglo-American relations, all he has to do is let me know."

"He wants you back in America."

"It's a short-term assignment. I'm leaving in three weeks anyway."

"What are you doing today?" he asked as I turned to leave.

"I'm selling secrets to the Russians."

As I walked away from the coffee shop, Dan caught my departure on a series of photographs. As I travelled further into the distance, he returned his camera's view to Adam Lewis.

Dan lost sight of me for twenty seconds.

It took him ten minutes to find me again.

I paused and rubbed at my leg. This was the furthest I had walked in one day in a long time and I'd pushed it too far. The pain was getting worse with each step. I leaned against a wall and tried to shift my weight temporarily to my left side. I swallowed a couple of emergency pills that I carried for unforeseen emergencies and immediately exceeded the daily recommended dosage.

My phone rang.

"Hello."

"This is the president."

It was Dan Jackson.

"Did he follow?"

"He stayed in the coffee shop, but you are being followed. Two men, unknowns, unprofessional. I think you're about to be mugged."

Kit inspected the computer store's hardware. He has a weakness for gadgets and accessories that may one day spiral out of control. He answered his ringing phone.

"Hello."

"Nick's in danger." Ben said.

"Where is he?"

My top speed isn't what it used to be. Four men continued to follow me at a distance. They'd tried to disguise their increased numbers, but my pitiful rate of acceleration had clearly confused their tactics. They were gaining.

I tried to keep my composure, more for the benefit of the trainee who was watching my every move, but I was genuinely worried. The pain was increasing. My phone rang again.

"It's the president. They're still following. Do you want me to intervene?"

"No, keep your distance. This is too big a coincidence. Keep watching. Tell Maggie to meet me at the operation's back-up location."

"You are five minutes away. You won't make it before they catch up."

"Tell Maggie to secure line of sight. If I'm attacked on a crowded street, it's a street crime. If you *prevent* an attack on me on a crowded street, it's an incident, an investigation and a recall. Where is Kit?"

Kit sprinted down the street, weaving in and out of the people. He was ten minutes away. The four men continued to gain. Dan abandoned his viewing point and tailed my would-be attackers. He looked behind him, hoping to see Kit. My best friend was nowhere in sight.

I was in agony and limping badly. My phone rang again.

"You're not going to make it before they intercept." Dan said.

"Where is Kit?"

"I don't know!"

Kit selected a speed dial number on his phone without reducing his speed. He almost collided with some tourists as he clumsily made the selection.

"Dan, I won't be there in time. You need to get involved."

"He told me to keep my distance."

"Ignore the order. Get involved!"

I reached a straight, narrow alley and turned sharply into it. The high walls on either side hid me from the public and kept the area in shadow. The alley ended at the service entrance for a hotel, our agreed meeting place. Fifty short metres to safety. I wouldn't make it.

I grabbed onto anything that could provide temporary support as I stumbled along the narrow route. The group of four gained on me easily. Three of them casually produced a hidden weapon, a collection of metal bars and clubs. I made it halfway along the alley before I collapsed.

I lay on the ground for a few moments and regained my breath. I finally sat up as the gang surrounded me.

Despite their height and build, they shared almost nothing else in common. I silently congratulated them on being such a politically correct, ethnically diverse group of criminals.

The tallest of the men produced a bicycle chain from his pocket instead of the knife I'd expected. This told me three things. It told me that their intent was to seriously injure but not kill me. More importantly, they had absolutely no idea who they were dealing with. Somebody had given them my face and my location and forgotten to mention my occupation. Finally, it suggested that there was bike somewhere that didn't work as well as intended.

"That was fun, wasn't it?" I said. "I like games. Do you like games?"

They didn't reply.

"My favourite game's called Five Seconds. Did you ever play a game called Five Seconds?"

They didn't reply.

I waited to see which of the men would step forward. Eventually the man with the bicycle chain did so. I proceeded to explain the rules of my game to him.

"It's really simple. I start with a question. I ask you something like 'who hired you?'..."

Three bullets flew towards us. The three men standing behind their leader collapsed, each one the victim of a non-fatal wound to the shoulder. He glanced backwards as they fell, confused as to why they'd fallen. In the moment that granted me, I drew a gun from my ankle, pointed it at his face and finished the rules to my game.

"... and you get five seconds."

Maggie disassembled her sniper rifle and returned it to an innocuous canvas bag. By the time she reached Ben's waiting car, I had Adam Lewis' name.

At some point, I'm not entirely sure when, I started to equate cricket with Conrad Dean. It's not simply that he is a fan, although he is. It's not only that it's pretentious and arguably pointless. It's simply that both act as if they are a favourite of the nation, when for every fan they delight, there's another person they irritate and another two they bore. I thought my negative opinion of cricket might generate a reaction from the Englishmen I know, but many of them agree with me.

Adam Lewis supports a soccer team called Tottenham, but his favourite sport is Rugby. I have nothing bad to say about rugby. The people I know who play it, watch it and love it are monsters of men and I respect the right of violent, scary people to watch whatever sport they wish. I feel the same way about my American colleagues who watch, love and train in mixed martial arts.

Adam tried half-heartedly to persuade the four criminals to press charges. They declined. None of them could think of a plausible reason that explained their presence in the alley and all had criminal records for assaulting tourists. Adam meekly accepted their decision. I didn't know this at the time and he decided to make use of that.

The day after the attack, Ed Williams intercepted me in the main foyer of The Old House and delivered some priority mail. I opened it and pulled out a piece of plain, nondescript paper. On the page was one sentence.

"I can prove you were involved."

The next day, Conrad and Adam were intercepted by Conrad's personal assistant, Gina Martin. Gina is so pretty that it raises serious questions about the reasons for her recruitment. She passed them a piece of priority mail, addressed to them both.

Adam Lewis accepted it suspiciously and opened it to find the same note inside. He turned it over and found the new message I'd scrawled on the other side.

"Anything you can prove, I can prove better. I can prove anything better than you."

On Sunday evening, I left through the front gate of The Old House. I had vague plans to breathe fresh air and see the sky. My real motive was to determine what British Intelligence would say if they had an opportunity to speak to me. I made it thirty feet before a black cab slowly drifted towards me. Simon Walker smiled from inside.

He took me to a local bar, an old-fashioned pub with nineteen less televisions than I was used to. The server tracked down some American beer in bottles that no one else had requested in weeks. Simon kindly agreed to drink the same, but he struggled to hide his disappointment when he tasted it.

"You look like something is troubling you." I said.

I meant the beer, but he thought I was talking about his invitation.

"I've been asked to look into something and I've got to waste my time because of who asked. I figure, if you tell me the story, I'll write it up and we can both move on."

"You're going to ask me if I sold secrets to the Russians." I guessed.

"It's a joke. I know it's a joke. But talking about Russians to some people is like saying you put a bomb in your luggage and hoping the airline thinks it's funny. If you say it, we have to check it."

"It's a training exercise. I'm a traitor. I have a colleague playing it Russian; nostalgic I guess. We've got trainees trying to catch us passing documents."

"Thanks. That'll save me time."

We drank some more beer and he pulled some more faces.

"What do you think of Britain?" he asked.

"I hate your food, I hate your weather, I hate your television and I hate your sports. Yet, for reasons I can't fully explain, I love it here."

"America's not known for its contribution to world cuisine."

"I didn't say it was. I live on Mexican and pizza. You?"

"Mostly Chinese and the occasional curry. I won't argue weather with you."

"That's for the best. It's raining again."

"But I've got to defend sport. We gave sport to the world."

"And the world keeps beating you at it. Talk about ingratitude."

"I'm not sure I should take abuse from a country that acts so smug about being the best at sports it invented and the rest of the world ignores."

"If the world doesn't see the greatness in baseball, that's the world's problem, not mine."

"Doesn't baseball drag for three hours?"

"Doesn't cricket drag for five days?"

"I suppose so. Anyway, we do play baseball, except it's called Rounders and it's popular with eight year old girls."

"I'm laughing so hard on the inside that my lungs just swapped places. I've heard that joke so many times, I'm starting to wonder if you're forced to recite it at school. Do you know who plays soccer? It's the unfortunates too short for basketball, too slow for hockey, too dumb for baseball and too scared for football. I don't get the British obsession with sports. Why be so dedicated to something in which you are eternally destined to fail? It's a recipe for misery."

"At least we're good losers."

"You get more practise then we do."

"Big-headed Yank."

"Whiny Brit."

We both grinned. It's fair to say I like him a lot.

It was while I was enjoying my evening out that Adam Lewis plotted a covert route onto Conrad Dean's tree-lined avenue. He passed the multi-million pound homes and expensive cars until he reached Dean's Jaguar. He pulled a brick from one pocket and a knife from the other.

Simon Walker dropped me outside The Old House and I heard the argument before I saw it. I hesitated outside the main door until I could determine what I was about to walk into.

"I don't care if you are the president." Leah yelled at Maggie. "Get him out here right now."

Kit appeared from the basement door to investigate the raised voices.

"Leah, what's the problem?"

"If I speak of the devil, I expect him to appear, not send a junior demon to take a message."

"I told her Nick is out." Maggie explained to Kit.

"I'm back now." I said as I entered the foyer.

"What did you do?" Leah asked angrily.

"What is it you think I did?" I replied.

"You were seen, Nick. You were seen scratching Conrad's car, slashing its tyres, smashing its windows. And you promised me. You promised me low profile. You promised no scandals."

"Conrad Dean has a secret service liaison called Adam Lewis." I explained calmly. "Tell him to speak to Simon Walker. Simon's my alibi for the evening and I can't be in two places at once. If they drop this accusation, I won't make a formal, diplomatic complaint of harassment. ... You've stopped shouting. Good. Don't ever come here with unconfirmed accusations. Maggie, show her out."

I entered the basement slowly. I picked up a cup from Kit's desk and hurled it against the nearest wall, smashing the mug and coating the wall in cold coffee.

"What did you do?" Conrad asked quietly.

He was careful of his volume. He was visibly furious in every other way.

"I don't know what you mean."

"You had an idea for implicating Hadley in a crime. I said I didn't need to hear it and then ... My car was a work of art. My car was a thing of beauty."

"We'll catch whoever did it." Adam replied, deadpan.

"Maybe it's time I spoke with your department."

"And tell them *what*?"

"We argued. You threatened me. You threatened to damage my car."

"If you speak to my people, I speak to the press."

"And tell them *what*?"

"You're cheating on your wife. ... You are cheating on her, aren't you? Did you really think I hadn't worked that out? I guess that would hurt your career. Oh, maybe end your marriage too."

Conrad Dean didn't reply.

"Our deal is done." Adam said. "Pay the amount we agreed and arrange my transfer back to my old role."

"What about Hadley?"

"He's about to leave. He won. You lost. Let him go."

We met for our regular Monday meeting. The basement was quieter than normal and Todd looked exhausted. He'd stayed awake all night, hacking the systems of soccer's governing bodies. He believed that the busier he kept them, the less they would notice a little, south coast club.

I entered the room and the energy immediately improved. I can't take all the credit. Most of the people here liked to cause trouble and I continued to give them that opportunity.

I spoke to Ben first because he sported one of the room's few smiles.

"Ben, what do you have for us?"

"Chemical B passed the test."

"Which one's B?"

"It's bad for grass. Good teams play passing football. They can't do that if we ruin their grass. And we have an idea for how we can get it into sprinkler systems. They'll kill their own pitch and they'll never know we helped."

"Where do we start?"

"I say we start in London and target Frank, Tony, Ossie and Trevor."

I approved the project. I sometimes made suggestions, but I rarely blocked anything. Every time we met as a group, I felt like an ill-disciplined child in a candy store. I wanted everything.

After the meeting finished, Ed smuggled me out of The Old House and I visited with Leah for my bi-weekly lie to the embassy. Leah seemed distracted. I knew it was serious when we were ten minutes into the meal and she still hadn't initiated an argument.

"Bad day?"

She hesitated. For reasons I've explained, I'm not her first choice for a sympathetic ear. She agreed anyway, too tired to fight me.

"It's not often, but … sometimes people leave me out. It's selective memory. They remember the part where I was investigated. They forget the part where I was cleared."

"Sorry."

"It's too easy to blame you. They've been told countless times that my clearance is restored. A year ago, it was your fault. But now? … I shouldn't admit this, but I'm not mad with you anymore. Between the shooting and my false accusations the other night, and it was six months ago, you know?"

I stayed quiet. She wanted to talk and I let her.

"I'm still upset with myself though." she admitted. "I knew you were a professional liar. I knew that, and then I believed everything you told me."

"I'm a great liar." I admitted.

"Don't sound so proud about it."

"Professionally, it's helpful, I won't deny it. But personally, it's bad news when people who matter don't trust you. And the truth is, I never lied to you about you. I made a mistake, and it was a huge mistake, but I did it because I cared about you."

"I know. And I know you'd like to start over, but we can't."

"Why not?"

"Everything we had was built on a lie. It all collapsed the moment I learned the truth."

"What if I stopped lying permanently?"

"Didn't you admit that lying is an important part of what you do?"

"I'll quit." I said.

"As simple as that?"

"If I had to make a choice right now between you and my work, I would choose you."

She paused and considered my offer.

"I'm sorry. I don't believe you."

Adam Lewis hailed a passing black cab. It slowed down and he climbed in.

"What's your part in all this?" he asked the driver.

Simon Walker pulled away from the curb and into the slow loving traffic.

"I'm an interested observer."

"If you were just an observer, this would be a phone call."

"A week ago, I gave an alibi to a suspect for the alterations on your best pal's Jag. I think it's a stroke of luck because it stopped you chasing the wrong man. Instead, it plays like I'm the bad guy for backing his story. Now, I think I did you a favour. You think I caused a problem. I don't get that ... unless it was you who smashed up the car?"

Adam replied, but ignored the question.

"I wanted it to be Hadley because it would have made my life easier. You did us a favour, but I was disappointed. There's no bad feeling. I'm sorry it seemed that way."

"Apology accepted."

Walker broke from the conversation to swear at an aggressive driver attempting to push into a non-existent gap.

"You spoke with Hadley." Lewis said. "Why do you think he came back?"

"He's running a training op for some new recruits. We're guessing he's been dropped a few levels, maybe because he upsets the top people in the States the same way he upsets them here."

"They run training in a lot of countries. Why London?"

"I don't know," Walker said. "but if someone signed a death warrant on me, I'd want to be where I could find out who signed it."

Todd and Kit stopped talking as I entered the basement. There must have been something in my face that suggested my story was more interesting than their discussion.

"Good meeting?" Kit asked.

"I'm a manipulative, compulsive liar with an inability to change and no hope of being trusted by anybody ever again."

"Ouch. She said that?"

"It was implied. Let's change the subject."

Todd grinned maniacally and I'd guessed he'd done something sneaky and evil.

"I'm afraid to ask."

"I've rerouted Niall's bonus payments into the wrong accounts. It'll take months for anyone to work out where they've gone. If Niall checks his accounts, the transfers will look right, except the players won't have their money. Now, if we start a rumour that Niall is deliberately stalling on bonuses and the players check with their banks ..."

"You're a menace to society." I told him.

I can't describe how delighted I was that he was our menace.

This wasn't our only recent success. We'd persuaded some of soccer's best doctors and physios to ply their trade in America for significant raises. We'd triggered an argument between a rival team's coach and the referee's association that had the potential to influence decisions during the season. We'd intercepted scouting reports and, on one occasion, influenced its translation.

The simplest and most frequent of our schemes was our acquisition and distribution of confidential information. These pieces of news included unhelpful rivalries between teammates, borderline extortion from sports agents, illegal bonuses and one chairman's slanderous remarks about his team's fans.

There were few limits to our potential influence and the behaviour at some clubs made our work easier than we ever could have imagined.

We met for our final Monday meeting. It was seven days before my return. It was two weeks before the start of the English soccer season.

We reviewed our progress so far, based on the stories in that morning's sports pages. Ivan Hasek had rejected a move to Manchester United after question marks over his fitness. Arsenal's pre-season schedule had been disrupted yet again, this time by a bomb scare near their ground. A collection of Chelsea's players had fallen victim to a flu bug sweeping their squad. The dispute over TV money was showing no signs of a conclusion. Garcia, the Argentinean winger, was about to join Real Madrid as the most expensive seventeen year-old ever. Manchester City had admitted to tensions in their squad over shirt numbers after refuting the story for the previous month. Finally, four separate clubs had unveiled plans to replace their pitch before the season even started.

In other news, tucked away in the small print, bookmakers continued to slash the odds of Erich Maier lifting a trophy. The unlikely event was being backed heavily in the Far East following the arrival of some star names.

The papers concluded that it was a bad time to run an English football club. Nobody hinted that there might be other powers at play. Nobody suspected that we were those powers.

At the same time that our plans were showing progress, Adam's schemes were returning to haunt him. The men he'd hired to scare me wanted money for their silence. Adam needed a smooth transition back to his old department and he agreed to meet them.

He drove to an abandoned factory, a place they'd used several times before. Adam handed across the envelope of money immediately.

"I'm sorry for what happened. This works out to treble what I promised."

"It's not enough." the thug replied.

People stepped out from every direction and headed towards Adam.

"Don't do this." Lewis said. "There has to be a way to fix this."

"There is. Give me someone else to blame. Then give me their address"

I walked down the street, my every move captured by a quick succession of black and white photos. The pictures zoomed in with each successive shot, first to me and then to the envelope in my left hand. I paused. As I walked away, it wasn't clear if I still had the envelope or not.

Maggie sprinted into the street. She quickly reached the location where I'd hesitated. Dan photographed her arrival and her failure to find the parcel. A minute later, Ben confirmed that he'd lost sight of me. It was their final training mission and they'd missed both the drop and the pickup.

I'd adopted different strategies each Friday. The final test was all about Evelyn. She makes it look easy. For her, it is easy.

I met up with them in the basement. Maggie, Dan and Ben all looked disappointed. They're sore losers and I'm OK with that. With this attitude, and their incredible skill sets, I'm predicting they're going to win a lot.

"You did well." I told them. "You kept with me longer than I would have liked. And you were never going to see Evelyn."

"We know that." Maggie complained. "We don't have to like it."

"And that's OK if you let it motivate you in the right way. I'm proud of you all. Take the night off. Have some fun."

They accepted my offer. To my surprise, Todd declined an invitation to join me for dinner at Evelyn's apartment and decided to go for a drink with The Presidents instead.

Ed drove Kit and me to the other side of the city. Kit rode shotgun. I hid in the trunk. McRae arrived before us and we sat around a spectacular meal that Evelyn had prepared. In addition to her other skills, she's also an incredible cook. I've never heard a rational explanation for why my father divorced her.

"When do you fly home?" McRae asked me.

"I'll go stateside soon. So will Evelyn and Todd. Kit is staying in London, so if you need help later in the year, contact him."

"With everything that has happened, I can't wait to see if we'll win."

"Does the dishonesty bother you?" Kit asked.

"I like winning." McRae admitted. "Does it bother you?"

"We work for the US government." Evelyn replied. "Dishonesty hasn't troubled us in years."

My phone rang. I excused myself from the table and answered it.

"Hello."

"Meet me at The House." Leah said.

It wasn't a request.

Ben, Dan, Maggie and Todd sat around a table while a live jazz band played at the far end of the room. Todd drank more than usual and tried to hide his jealousy as Ben and Dan flirted harmlessly with Maggie. Their proven ability to impress women and their failure to seduce Maggie was an established joke among the three.

"You're not the gift to women that you think you are." Maggie told Dan.

"I could make you leave here with me in two sentences." Dan said.

Maggie was sceptical. Dan leaned over and whispered in her ear.

"That's not bad." she admitted.

Ben leaned across and whispered in her other ear. Maggie visibly blushed and looked at Todd.

"What about you? Two sentences."

Todd didn't want to be part of the conversation, but everyone was looking at him. He looked at the cellar they'd entered and thought about how much she'd enjoyed her evening.

"Do you like this place?"

"Yes, I do."

"Do you want me to buy it for you?"

Ben and Dan smirked derisively, but Maggie smiled.

"No, trust me." she said. "That works."

Todd's phone rang.

Everything in the basement was destroyed. The intruders had smashed computers. They'd shattered and scattered pieces of furniture. All that remained in the side office I'd converted into a bedroom were the ashes of a fire that no longer burned.

"Who was behind this?" Leah asked me.

"I've got an idea, but I can't prove it."

"Conrad Dean?"

"He wants a scandal and an inquiry and he wants me out. Is he going to get it? Is that why you're here?"

"I didn't come here for that. I was coming over anyway. I have bad news."

"More bad news. That's great. Wait, don't tell me. Let me guess. When you called, you were here already. You wanted to tell me the news personally. It's news that came through your sources faster than mine. It's news that couldn't wait until tomorrow. … And you've got a look of sympathy that I … that I don't deserve after all I've done. …"

My speech slowed and my expression switched from defensive to stunned as I solved the puzzle.

"He's dead, isn't he?"

"I'm sorry. We're hearing too many rumours."

"Heart attack?"

"They think so."

Kit entered.

"Nick, I spoke to the police. They canvassed the area and they've … What?"

"It's Silas. … Leah, will they recall?"

"Not yet. Nothing's official."

"Can you get me on an available flight?"

"It's arranged. It leaves in two hours."

Maggie, Todd, Ben and Dan entered the room. Todd looked solemn. Maggie, Ben and Dan looked tired and confused.

"I'm glad you're here. I wanted to tell you all that your work has been of the highest standard and I wanted to say goodbye. I promise you that whatever you do next, wherever you go, your references from me will be among the best you ever receive. I plan to sing your praises to anyone who will listen."

"I don't understand." Dan said.

"After this attack on our base, they'll want me to make a report in person." I said. "But we're receiving word that Silas Gower, the senior operations manager who approved my transfer here, has died. His successor won't authorize my return."

"So, don't leave. Wait for them to pull you out."

"It's not that simple. Silas Gower was my father. ... Our project wasn't supposed ... It wasn't supposed to end this way. I'm sorry for ... I'm just sorry."

Ed Williams drove me to the airport. I looked out of the window distractedly. I barely registered the famous landmarks we passed on our journey.

Leah travelled with me and we shared the back seat. I appreciated the gesture, but I paid her less attention than she deserved for most of the ride. I was already five times zones away.

"It's going to be quiet around here without you." Leah said.

"I could try and cause an incident from America." I replied.

"It wouldn't be the same."

We both attempted to smile.

"Did you know Silas was a fan of yours?" I said. "He met you at an official function."

"Eight years ago. I remember."

"He came to visit me at the hospital after I was shot. We had one of those awkward conversations were he tried to be my father instead of a department head and then didn't know what to say. I told him we'd met, not that I liked you or was spending time with you, only that we'd met. He said 'She's too smart for you'. I got defensive. '*I'm* smart' I said. He looked at me, smiled, and told me 'She's smarter. Trust me. I'm smarter than you too'."

"He was a good man."

"I don't know about that," I said. "but he was something."

I meant it as a compliment. Silas would have understood.

What I Did When I Wasn't Saving the World (Part 3)

I don't want to tell you about the eight or so months that followed my flight out of England. I attended a funeral. I survived an internal investigation into the attack on the Old House. I returned to my old responsibilities and the mundane tasks that they give to deskbound field agents.

If that sounds like insufficient activity to fill eight months, I assure you that it felt that way too.

Back in England, The Presidents had rejected transfers to other countries and other projects for the chance to work with Kit and stay together. Their career prospects improved with every passing week, while Kit somehow escaped credit for any of their successes.

Southampton had slumped from early success and fallen to third in the league. They were due to appear in the cup final after a series of home ties against struggling opposition. I suspected Kit's involvement in the draws that determined the favourable fixtures. I imagine that the woes of the lower league clubs were coincidences he was merely exploiting.

Southampton's year had gone well but not well enough. I knew the feeling.

A colleague placed some files on my desk. I glanced at them, gazed out of the window, returned briefly to the files and then gazed out the window some more. I considered taking a nap as part of a scientific study, the end result of which would be to determine the consequences of such an act. I'd recently been curious.

I was rescued from my pointless deliberations by a ringing phone.

I entered Todd's office. It was untidier than ever. As Todd saw me, he immediately flicked the privacy switch on the black box behind him. In the absence of another chair, I sat down on the floor against the far wall.

"I'm really glad you called." I said. "They've got me working child's play and I was about to drift into coma."

"They don't pull that with me because I know what shares they've bought."

I apologized for not visiting. I accompanied it with a lame excuse that neither of us believed. He kindly proposed a shared responsibility for the failure.

"Thank you for what you said in your report. You made me sound like a saint." Todd said.

"Get any benefit from that?"

"Yeah, I was well regarded for at least a few weeks. How are you?"

"How am I? That's a tough one. I wanted to put right everything I got wrong. Instead, I rely on pain medication to complete everyday tasks. My ex still rarely speaks to me. Kit's career is still a mess. I've broken the last promises I made to my dying father. My thank you to the guy who saved my life is going to fail. Oh, and I hate my job. Other than that, I'm OK. ... Sorry. You said you wanted to know."

"Yeah, my mistake. I'll be more careful in future."

"When you called, you said you needed help. Are you in some kind of trouble?"

"We both are. We're both in some kind of trouble."

"What kind?"

"The kind where you steal 499 million from an authorized project with no start date and then it receives one. We've got three weeks to put the money back."

I walked into my father's old office. They'd painted it to a different colour scheme and sturdy bookcases dominated every wall. Every case was stacked full of large, reference books.

Zachary Bristow, the new head of department, glanced upwards with only a cursory acknowledgement of my entrance. He looked busy and stressed. He always looks busy and stressed

He hates me, not for any single, significant reason, but for a million little things, most of which are unjustified. I won't criticize this decision; I dislike him for similarly flawed reasons. Our personalities collide head on with sufficient force to write off both vehicles and injure the drivers.

"I like the room's new look." I said. "Have you read all these books?"

"No, there were too many long words and not enough pictures. What do you want Nick? I'm busy. Ask. Let me say no and put you out of my misery."

"I'd like to check on the agents I mentored in England."

"You managed three months without starting a war, but little else has changed. We may not like some of their people, but we have to work with them. You make that work complicated."

"Is that the only reason?"

"No, I don't like you and it amuses me that you only receive boring assignments."

"I'll make it worth your while."

"You have nothing I want."

Ed Williams met me as I exited Heathrow airport. He kindly took some of my bags and we walked towards his waiting car.

"I didn't think you'd be back."

"I'm persuasive." I said.

Ed's phone rang. He looked at the number and handed it to me as soon as he recognised it.

"You're back." Leah said in a tone that suggested she didn't hate the fact. "What's your fictitious cover for being here this time?"

"I wanted to deliver your birthday present personally." I replied. "I think you'll like it. It's what you want more than anything else in the world."

"You've already been shot. You moved back to America. I'm not sure what else is left."

"It's good to talk to you too."

"Are you going to behave?"

"As close as I ever get."

I walked through The Old House's main entrance and Kit greeted me immediately. We talked as we walked towards the doorway at the back of the lobby.

"I was surprised when you called."

"I made you all a promise and I won't give up until I put right everything that's wrong in this world."

"That could take a while."

"I'm going to start with everything that's wrong because of me and I've only got 18 days."

"You're going to need help."

"Who did you have in mind?"

I looked into a well-lit, custom designed project space. It was unrecognizable from the dark hole we'd conspired in months earlier. Leaning against the new furniture were The Presidents and Todd Perry.

Gina, Conrad's assistant, showed Adam Lewis into the politician's office and offered him a drink. He accepted a seat and declined the coffee. Conrad bustled in moments later, an escapee from a committee he was supposed to be chairing.

"Adam. Thank you agreeing to see me."

"Congratulations on your promotion."

"Nothing is official yet and there may be a problem."

Adam could predict Conrad's complaint and attempted to excuse himself from any possible solution.

"I don't work for you anymore."

"I could make it worth your while, like old times."

"I'm back in my old role. Things are going well. Why would I spoil that?"

"I'll pay you twice as much as last time. ... And I only want to know why he's back."

"... That's all?"

"That's all."

Kit and I sat in a corner while the others went in search of a celebratory meal to mark my return. While we waited for the arrival of the take-out, Kit summarized the details of the previous eight months.

"Good, really good, but not good enough." he said. "We're looking at second place and that would be a problem."

"What happened?"

"We had some success. The internal disagreements we started at Niall compromised their entire year. The flu bug hit Frank more than the others and they struggled to catch up after it derailed their first two months. Gary and Ossie both had the seasons we expected and finished higher mid-table. Bruce intermittently dropped points against teams you would expect them to beat and couldn't maintain enough of a run to mount a challenge."

"How did you arrange that last one?"

"We didn't. Apparently they do that sometimes."

"That leaves Bryan and Tony."

Kit nodded his agreement.

"We started well. We led at Christmas. Then we got injuries midseason, lost our confidence away from home, took a bad run in March."

"Bryan?"

"We blocked their transfers, but they brought in talented youngsters. We hit their finances, but they bounced back with new deals. We set the governing bodies against them, but it unified them and improved team spirit. Oh, and the guy we hypnotized to stop scoring set a record for the most assists in a single season."

"Tony?"

"They went on a run as we hit our rough patch and their home form has been great all season."

I did the math in my head, but I asked Kit for his calculations.

"What now? Assume I don't already know."

"There is one game to go. We're three points behind both Bryan and Tony. We'll win our remaining game. That puts us level, with a superior goal difference, if Bryan and Tony fail to get any more points."

"And they play each other in their final league game."

"We can get 77. If Bryan or Tony wins, they reach 80. If they draw, they both move to 78. Whatever happens, we're at least a point behind."

I paused to think through the problem. I started to smile. It was an evil smile, worthy of Todd Perry.

"I want to speak to McRae. We need to know if there's any precedent in English football for point deduction."

Conrad saw Adam Lewis loitering by the side of the corridor and walked towards him.

"What did you find out?" Conrad whispered.

"Nobody knows why he's back."

"There must be a reason, even if it's a cover."

"We have a source ideally placed for this kind of information." Adam revealed. "There is no explanation for his return, not even a lie."

I sat in a circle with Kit, Todd and Ben. Our discussion was already in full-flow. We had a solution from our insider and Ben had the expertise. Todd explained it for our young colleague.

"If we cause a brawl between the opposing players, the governing body will be forced to deduct points from the teams."

"We need to start a fight?" Ben asked.

"Not any fight. We need stewards to throw punches. We need substitutes breaking noses. We need cops injured as they drag players apart. And I think that you know how to get it."

"You're talking about the grass attack."

Ben had conned four different clubs into spraying grass-killing chemicals onto their own pitches using sprinkler systems. Last time, they'd ruined the grass. If Ben varied the chemical, he could orchestrate temporary psychosis and associated violence.

"Can you do it?" I asked.

"I can do it." Ben replied confidently. "The hardest part will be deciding how bad the fight should be."

The final weekend of the league season, every match was scheduled for the same start time. It was arranged this way to ensure that no club had an advantage over the others. All of these precautions proved irrelevant because one of the games never finished.

The first scuffle started before the first whistle. The first punch landed after two. The first brawl sparked after four minutes. They abandoned the game after eight.

On reflection, we might have gone a little heavy on the chemicals.

I hadn't spoken to McRae since my return to Britain. However, Evelyn was back in England as part of a mission whose details reside above my pay grade and she had acted as an intermediary to an on-going conversation. We arranged to meet and settled on the middle of the night, the only time he could escape from the celebrations without causing suspicion.

The moment he entered Evelyn's apartment and saw me, he grinned like a teenager who'd discovered the joys of vandalism. I attempted to shake his hand. He pulled me into a tight hug like an old friend. Apparently this happens when you help someone's dream become a reality.

"Congratulations on your team's league title." I said.

He finally released me, but his grin didn't fade. I smiled too. I couldn't help it.

"Did you think we'd do it?" I asked McRae.

"I told myself 'Yes', but I secretly thought 'No'."

"I knew you'd do it." Evelyn told me. "I'm a hopeless optimist."

When you win as frequently as Evelyn does, optimism is probably inevitable.

"I'm an eternal pessimist." McRae admitted. "In business, anything can happen, and in sport …"

We took two of the available seats at the table and Evelyn joined us. She passed us each a glass of wine and poured a generous portion for herself.

"Do you feel like you know football now?" McRae asked me.

"I'm getting there. I know your teams and players. I understand the rules. I instinctively look for Saturday results. I call it football instead of soccer. What am I missing?"

"Where do I start? You don't know why 96 minutes is called Fergie Time. You won't know where you were when England beat Germany 5-1. You can't tell me what's special about Russian linesmen. *And* you've never set foot inside a football stadium."

"OK, that's true."

I looked at Evelyn for support. Despite all the help she'd provided, she knew even less about the national institution we'd just manipulated than I did. Before we could discuss some next steps, McRae told us a joke.

"Manchester United and Manchester City played home games on the same weekday night. After the games, all the routes leading out of the city were jammed with traffic. A policeman was heard to say 'Our roads couldn't cope with three sets of away supporters.'"

"You've lost me."

"Sorry. You're not there yet."

"Life's too short and my heart belongs to baseball."

"We have baseball in this country." he said.

"Please, no, I've heard it and it wasn't funny the first time. Are you going to explain the Manchester story to me?"

"Two games and three sets of away supporters. It implies that everyone from Manchester supports City and all the United fans come from Kent and Surrey."

"I guess jokes don't work if you have to explain them."

"I guess not."

We all took a sip of our drinks, an expensive red that Evelyn had selected. It took a few moments for my brain to appreciate the joke's importance.

"... Kent and Surrey. They're in the southeast, right?"

Kit was asleep when I called. He was semi-conscious when he answered.

"Do you want to hear a story about away supporters?" I said.

"What time is it?"

"It's two-thirty? Do you want to hear the joke?"

"No, I want to be asleep."

"Then I'll cut to my favourite line. Everyone from Manchester supports City and United fans come from Kent and Surrey."

"I don't get it."

"That's OK. It's probably not true anyway, but that's not important. What is important is that there were two games on the night I was shot. Arsenal played Chelsea and Newcastle played Manchester. We knew he was stuck in traffic. We assumed he was stuck in London traffic."

Kit woke up.

Dan climbed the high wall surrounding the meticulously maintained and very private golf course. He crept through the trees until he had a view of the twelfth hole. We watched his line of sight from the comfort of a monitor in The Old House's basement.

Three men watched a fourth prepare to tee off down the fairway that ran past Dan's covert position.

"Which one?" I asked Kit.

"The tall one at the back. He's a law-abiding, legitimate businessman with links to the rich and powerful."

"Who are the others?"

"They're his bad influence. The four of them are co-directors in at least one company and co-owners of a corporate box in a certain Manchester soccer stadium. And they all possess affluence that their legal enterprises don't entirely explain."

"They'd have to be to play golf here without climbing a wall." Dan mumbled into his headset.

"Is he the one who called the hit?" I asked.

"We think so."

The man teed off. His technique was excellent and his ball approached the green of a par 4.

"What do you want to do?" Kit asked me.

"I want to kill him. ... But I think we can be more creative."

I looked through a series of photographs, copies of the images Dan had captured at the golf course. The room was silent except for furious typing from Kit's computer. We needed confirmation and all possible responses were on hold until Kit obtained it.

Maggie entered the basement and approached my desk.

"You were right about Adam Lewis. He's desperate to find out why you're back in the country."

"Good. We can use that."

"That's not all. There's a rumour that Conrad Dean paid Lewis to keep a secret. I know it's an obvious leap, but could Conrad be cheating on his wife?"

"If it's true, I can guess who with."

As she left, Todd entered. She smiled sweetly and he smiled back. Todd dragged a chair from a nearby desk and sat opposite. I raised an eyebrow to his happy expression.

"Inter-team camaraderie." he explained unconvincingly

I noticed that his clothes were ironed and his beard was neater than the day before. I noticed primarily because he'd made so little effort previously. He changed the subject quickly.

"I know you have a lot to worry about, but we need to talk about the problem."

"Which one?" Kit and I answered in spontaneous harmony, proof that Kit was listening despite his research.

"I helped you steal money and we need to give it back before anyone realises it's gone."

I called Kit over and he joined us, bringing his chair with him.

"What do you know about stocks and shares?" I asked Todd.

"I know everything about them and you know that, but I can't get you 499 million."

"We don't need 499 million." Kit said. "We need 4 million."

"It still can't be done. It's gambling, only with companies instead of cards. The first rule of gambling is that the house always wins. This is no different. We can't take it for 4 million on this timeframe."

"You're forgetting something." I interrupted. "Gambling isn't good days and bad days; it's good players and bad players. We can win big if someone else loses big."

"Did you have someone in mind?"

I threw images from the golf course onto the desk and they scattered towards Todd. The top picture rotated and settled directly in front of him. I pretended it was planned, but it was a perfect execution I couldn't have repeated with a thousand attempts.

My luck was changing. I could feel it. There was no stopping me.

Conrad and Adam stepped into the shadows and lowered their voices.

"Somebody is asking questions about our previous business arrangement." Adam said. "I don't know what they've found out."

"What does that mean?"

"You wanted to know why Hadley was back in the country. I think he's coming after you."

We sent Maggie and Ben on pointless reconnaissance missions and sent Dan to watch who followed them. I wanted to know how closely we were under observation. We discovered that their tails were minimal. The British were still dedicating resources to my misbehaviour and very little to my team's.

Todd, Kit and I separated for a few minutes and returned with drinks. We huddled around my computer and awaited Todd's interrogation.

"You need to level with me. I'm going to help you raise 4 million. We need 499. I don't want to hear that 495 million isn't much between friends, because I can promise it is."

Kit provided Todd with our explanation.

"Ten months ago, before Meier, before cup runs, we took ten million dollars, laundered it, and placed it with betting syndicates in the Far East. We split the money over locations and dates and bet on our team to win the league and cup double. There's so much gambling on results there that ours got lost in the mix. Evan Noah's team won the league. If they win the cup this Saturday, the bets come good and we get back fifty times the original stake."

"Is this the part where we discuss devaluing currencies?"

"I guess tens of millions aren't worth what they used to be." I joked.

Todd didn't laugh.

"You should have told me sooner. ... We're four million short?"

"And loose change."

I looked at Kit for the exact number.

"It's about 846,082 dollars." he said.

"OK, five million." said Todd. "You don't need a broker, you need a thief."

I nodded to show we understood. I nodded to show we agreed. I even tried my best to appear remorseful, although I can't promise I was.

"You're right. You're right. We need a thief." I said. "... If only we knew one."

Todd ran the simulation for us, a kind and ultimately redundant courtesy. The collection of onscreen numbers made perfect sense to him and no sense to me. It was impressive and captivating and Kit's expression told me that he had no idea what he was looking at either.

"Let me explain." Todd said. "... What level?"

Kit provided a response on our behalf.

"Assume we're idiots."

"... OK. ... As you know, I deal in my spare time."

"How do you do?"

"Last year's profit was half a million. I'd quit the day job, but it's the source of all my best tips. Anyway, one of the reasons I'm so good is because I set up some software with an IT geek called Kris Khan."

"I know Kris." I said. "He's a smart guy."

"He's the smartest. Anyway, you put your companies into the software. You add your maximum buy price, minimum sell price, a few other parameters, and then hit Go. The software does the rest and it recognizes trends before they happen."

"How can we use it?"

"We pick companies with unstable share prices and start buying them. If we're aggressive enough, the price rises, people follow, and then we sell at the higher price. When we do, we've got so many shares that we'll trigger a price collapse. The problem is that if people are fast, and they are, we won't sell all our shares at the higher price. What we need is somebody with money and no brains whatsoever to keep buying the shares at the higher price and fail to see the imminent collapse."

"You make it sound easy."

"It isn't, but you asked for the idiot's guide. Kit got us confirmation that this is the guy who ordered your death. If you get me passwords, permissions, voice recognition, voice patterns, and get him away from his phone for two hours, I can do more than five million damage, and they'll never trace it back to us. And there's something else."

"What?"

"His dealing can go almost unlimited because he has an understanding with his bank and his bank has a connection with his business. His personal fortune is estimated at millions, but he's got more tied up in the company he co-owns with the bad guys from the golf course. If we hit past his fortune, we're going to take the company down too."

That was what I was hoping he'd say.

On the morning of the cup final, Adam Lewis parked on a crowded street, anonymous in the mass of traffic. He looked at the office towers in the distance as if it helped his concentration.

He debated the merits of ignoring Conrad's requests and forgetting I existed. He made a final decision and dialled a number on his mobile.

"Hello. It's me. I need some more information from your contact."

The bar was popular, crowded and trendy. Ed Williams liked the music they played and the female students who liked to drink there. He passed the bartender the payment for his drink. The bartender skilfully inserted a small piece of paper into the five pound note Ed received as change.

Five minutes later, Ed returned to The Old House and I intercepted him in the lobby. I tried to enlist his help without betraying anything confidential.

"Ed, we're running something this afternoon. We need another pair of hands, but I can't give you many details."

He tried to disguise the panic in his voice.

"That's OK. That's why I'm here."

"I want you to deliver a package."

I told him the time and place, and I passed him a parcel wrapped in brown paper.

"Consider it done."

"I need to keep this behind the embassy." I told him.

"That's not a problem." he replied.

He didn't speak a truer sentence that day. Ed was world-class at keeping secrets from the embassy.

He returned to his room at the top of The Old House, an attic whose tiny windows gave him spectacular views of the city. He locked the door and switched on his computer, a top of the range model perched on a table in the only clean corner of the room.

He placed the package on his bed and inspected the note from the bartender again. He hit the top of an old style stop clock and began to type quickly at his keyboard. He accessed one of the basement's computers using a trapdoor he'd established nine months earlier for emergencies. He navigated the files, links and icons without pausing, scanned it all without pausing to read. The clock counted down towards the thirty second mark.

He accessed a selection of titles from the basement's computers. He opened a folder called Permissions, viewed the contents briefly and closed it again. He opened a second folder called Reports, checked its files and closed this too. As the clock reached two minutes, he noticed a file called Dean.

He opened the folder's most recent file, memorized the address from its final paragraph and then exited our network. He wrote the location onto a small piece of paper and slid it into the lining of his sleeve.

As I entered the basement, Kit waved and called me over.

"My computer had a visitor." Kit whispered.

"Can you find out who it was?"

Kit shook his head.

"OK. Keep it to yourself."

I looked at Maggie and followed her line of sight to a large clock on the far wall. It was 10 minutes to three in the afternoon. It was 10 minutes until the cup final's kick-off.

Dan and Maggie glanced at me and I looked at Kit. Todd stared at his screen.

"Kit, how long do you need?" I said.

"I'm ready."

"You're sure."

"I'm ready. Let's do this."

I nodded to Maggie and Dan. They stood up and marched from the room.

"Make a call."

Kit picked up a headset and slid it over his head. He hit a key on his keyboard and it automatically triggered a number through his phone.

I counted to five slowly and then followed Dan and Maggie out of the basement.

Gina Martin, Conrad Dean's personal secretary, answered her cell. She'd tied her blonde hair back and she was power-dressed for an important meeting later that day.

"Hello. ... No, it isn't. I think you have the wrong number."

"My mistake." Kit replied. "I'm very sorry."

Kit typed a series of numbers into his computer and then violently tapped the return key as if every second were important.

Simon Walker parked his taxi a few hundred yards from The Old House. His car radio, tuned in for the soccer match, repeated the starting line-ups for the two competing teams.

Gina Martin selected a number from her phone's address book and nothing happened. She checked her main display and discovered she'd lost her signal.

Ben walked confidently through the tower's front entrance like he belonged. He glanced sideways as he passed the main desk. Its cameras missed him and the hassled receptionist was focused elsewhere. He climbed some rarely-used back stairs and entered an empty office.

Ten minutes after his arrival, he was hooked into the building's computer systems. A minute later, he crashed the entire phone system.

Simon Walker watched me leave the main gates of The Old House. The radio commentator announced the start of the match. Walker turned the key and prepared to follow.

Dan slowed down at a red light and Maggie climbed out of the passenger side. She ignored the high-end camera, the laptop and all the expensive gadgets, but picked up a small, carry-on case from the back seat. She closed the door again, tapped on the window and Dan drove away.

"Kit, it's Ben. They've lost land line. Kill their cell phones."

Leah reviewed the plans for an ambassador's arrival and found an anomaly. She cross-referenced the data with information she'd received the week before. The lists of attendees matched perfectly. The arrival dates disagreed by one day.

Kit played back a tape of his brief conversation with Gina Martin alongside some snippets of dialogue they had already obtained. He isolated her sentences and played them back repeatedly. He added distortion and the pre-recorded sounds of a bustling city, and the clarity of her voice disappeared into the mix. Kit typed new words and her voice repeated them in competition with the background noise.

Todd picked up a photograph of four men playing golf and taped it to his desk. He started the software application and numbers flashed across his screen. He told it to buy.

Gina Martin walked along the street, her phone raised above her head, in search of the signal she'd mysteriously lost.

I walked slowly away from our base of operations. I kept my natural pace, an unimpressive rate I select by default. It was slow enough that Simon Walker, through necessity, overtook me in his cab. He turned left and went in search of the next three left turns the one way system would allow.

Maggie unpacked her bag and pulled out a device. She pressed a clicker in her hand and the device flashed. She tested it three more times and then attached it to the hotel room's window, a view that faced out onto the gardens behind the building.

Conrad Dean stepped out of the meeting as soon as he recognized the phone number. He listened carefully, but the background noise made it difficult to decipher the message.

"I need … important."

"Gina. Is that? I can't hear you."

"... important ... our hotel."

Kit disconnected his call to Conrad. He hit the return key on his second computer and then turned briefly to face Todd.

"Tell Maggie he got the message."

Maggie, minus the jeans and T-shirt she'd arrived in, answered her phone. She'd draped a business suit on the bed nearby.

"He's on his way."

"I'm ready."

The four businessmen broke from their ill-tempered argument when one of them realized he'd lost his phone signal. He asked the others to check the sports news for him, but their phones couldn't help either.

Simon Walker glanced from side to side, but he couldn't see me. Eventually, hurried by an impatient driver behind him, he accelerated and drove on. His radio announced that Southampton had taken the lead with an early goal.

A short blonde with her hair tied back walked through the hotel lobby. She smiled for the hotel porters and hesitated near a corridor that led to the conference rooms.

I reappeared from a shop and carefully crossed the road. I looked from side to side to confirm I'd lost my pursuers. I cut between some stationary traffic and resumed my journey.

Ed parked alongside a vehicle with tinted windows. He climbed out of his car and carried the brown package with him. He opened the passenger door, placed it on the seat and closed the door again, a perfect recreation of my instructions. He didn't speak to the woman behind the wheel.

Evelyn waited until he'd left the area before she started the engine.

Conrad Dean walked through the hotel lobby quickly, eager to avoid any conversations. He saw a short lady with blonde hair disappear towards the conference rooms and followed her.

He continued down a maze of corridors, in pursuit of her confusing, weaving route. He exited the hotel into some gardens and reached out to grab her shoulder.

"I came as soon as I could."

Maggie turned to face him. She feigned shock and regained composure.

"I'm sorry. Do I know you?"

"No. No. You don't. Sorry."

Maggie squeezed something in her hand and triggered a series of bright flashes from behind her. Conrad instinctively assumed camera flashes and looked up at the light.

Maggie made her exit while he was distracted. She was through the door to the hotel before he recovered. She walked swiftly down the memorized path of corridors and pulled her cell phone from her pocket.

"It's done."

Leah pulled a printout from the original file and compared it to the two versions that had sparked her investigation. The original agreed with her copy, but the odd one out carried the most recent date. She went in search of the colleague who'd written it.

Conrad hid in a dark corner, huddled over his phone.

"I didn't call you." Gina told him. "My phone wasn't working until about a minute ago."

Adam Lewis's mobile vibrated in his pocket. He answered to a frantic Conrad Dean.

"Adam, name your price. You have to help me."

Evelyn drove between the warehouses and steered towards a collection of freight containers. The man coordinating the transfer of the merchandise into the nearest container opened the heavy door wider so that she could steer inside.

The four men exited the boardroom and approached some of their employees. The staff provided an update on the phone problems and promised a prompt return to service.

Ben tracked the traffic on the system and sent details to Kit. Five minutes later, the telephone repairman lost access to the system and his personal phone account disconnected.

The bartender passed Ed his usual drink. As Ed paid, he cleverly dragged his prewritten note and passed it to the bartender along with a ten pound note. The radio behind the bar announced another goal.

The bartender stepped into a back storeroom and picked up a phone.

Maggie switched back into her jeans and t-shirt. She packed away the business suit and the wig.

Todd flicked from database to database, through a long list of ever changing share prices. It was complex, it was evolving, but he understood it perfectly. He interrupted his purchases and authorised the start of the sale.

Evelyn climbed out of a different car and walked into the hangar. The small plane was waiting for her and the pilot had already placed her bags on board. As she walked towards the plane, she passed the brown package to the pilot. Inside was the payment they'd promised him.

Adam Lewis dialled a number from memory.

"I need to know what your guy discovered. … I don't care about the others. I need to know where to find Hadley."

Dan walked through the top level of a crumbling, multi-storey parking garage. He reached some pipes, a legacy of a previous need but abandoned as an eyesore. Behind the pipes was a hole where some workman had intended to complete some repairs. He pushed an envelope of photographs into the gap.

Ben left the office, his bag over his shoulder. Behind him, several people were shouting at an innocent, intimidated telephone repairman. As Ben left the building, the cameras missed him for a second time.

I glanced around, a final check for anyone who might be following. I saw nothing suspicious and left the stairwell of the garage. I approached the broken pipe and the hole it disguised.

The warehouse foreman waited until the final box was inside and then locked the container's doors. The land rover was buried under its other contents and became part of the export. The container carried the logo of McRae's company.

Ben jumped into his car and calmly re-joined traffic. He turned on the radio a moment after a Southampton effort that took it to 2-2.

Evelyn's plane left the runway and started its flight to France. She unofficially left a country she'd hadn't officially entered. There was no evidence of her arrival in England since her presence in London nine months earlier.

Todd inspected the information one last time and then stopped the application. He switched off his computer for good measure. He placed his feet on the ground and slowly wheeled himself backwards from the desk.

Kit and Todd looked at each other, hoping for confirmation of success.

"Did we do it?" Kit said.

"I think we did." Todd replied.

It was what Kit wanted to hear, but the tone of the response didn't convince him. Neither of them would believe in the victory until they heard it from me.

Four businessmen reclaimed their phone access five minutes after Ben's departure, thanks in part to a desperate and terrified repairman. Their cell phones refused to cooperate, but their land lines demanded their attention immediately. Their bank wanted to discuss the unsuccessful share dealing of four men who had started the morning as millionaires.

I retrieved the envelope from the hole behind the pipe work. It was exactly where I'd told Dan to leave it. I hesitated to reflect on my three young recruits and how much they'd impressed me.

I'd identified a hundred ways our plans might go wrong and I had seen us successfully skirt past most of them. More than ever, I was certain we had won.

The first blow struck my neck and head, a second hit my back. As I curled into a defensive shell, a third blow struck my side. My assailant picked up the envelope and walked away.

I didn't see his face.

I slowly, awkwardly tried to push myself up. My arms failed to support the weight and I collapsed face first into the uneven concrete.

Thirty minutes after the attack, Adam Lewis drove his car slowly down the road that sliced the urban park in two. He parked next to Conrad Dean. Adam stepped out of his black Land Rover and into Conrad's new Jaguar.

"Is that it?" Conrad asked.

Adam nodded and handed it across.

"Why give it to me?"

"It's your problem. I don't need to know what they are. You deal with them."

"What about your money?"

"Not now. I'll be in touch."

Conrad opened the envelope. As Adam opened the door and prepared to leave, Conrad pulled out photographs of Ed Williams passing documents to the unseen driver of a black Land Rover.

"I don't understand." Conrad said.

Seven cars accelerated towards them and screeched to a halt around the Jaguar. The final car to arrive was a black, London cab.

"What … What's happening?" Conrad asked.

Adam didn't respond to the question. He slumped into the passenger seat with resignation on his face. He guessed some of what had happened and he immediately admitted defeat. Fifteen British agents, led by Simon Walker, approached the car.

"Adam, I don't understand. What is this?" Conrad said.

"You said the Americans would finish you. They just did."

The agents led Conrad Dean and Adam Lewis towards two waiting cars. I watched the drama unfold from perfect seats, leaning against Walker's black cab. I was heavily bruised and ingesting some painkillers I kept for special occasions. As Conrad Dean walked past, he pretended he hadn't seen me. Adam Lewis wore the ironic smile of a gracious loser.

"You OK?" Lewis asked.

"I will be."

I appreciated the question. It was the decent thing to ask, even if he had inflicted the wounds I was nursing.

"I hear Americans are poor winners." he said, expecting me to gloat.

"I heard that too," I said. "but I'm only here to give you the news."

"What news?"

"I hear you're a Tottenham supporter. Southampton beat them with a last minute penalty."

I turned and walked away slowly. As I continued my departure, a nearby car radio repeated the news.

"... and Southampton football club have done it. They are the champions. They are the cup winners. They have completed the unlikeliest sporting triumph ever. ..."

Only when I'd travelled a respectable distance did I allow a smile to break across my face.

Leah didn't raise her voice at work often. Her tone could be so authoritative and convincing that increased volume wasn't typically required. This meeting was the exception. Her colleague squirmed guiltily as Leah asked increasingly difficult questions.

"Do you know something I don't?" Leah shouted.

"The arrival dates may change. ... They asked me to arrange it."

"Why wasn't I notified?"

Her colleague avoided eye contact.

"How long is this going to go on?" Leah said. "Yes, I was investigated. Of all people, I know I was investigated. And I was cleared of all charges. Which part of that is confusing? Which part of that do you fail to understand?"

Leah placed her documents into a folder and slammed it shut.

"Leah. Honestly, I ..."

"What I want more than anything in the world is for ..."

Her sentence trailed off. Something about the expression she'd used reminded her of the description I'd provided of her birthday present. Before she could collect her thoughts, her phone rang.

The interview room was sparse, lifeless. I watched Ed Williams through the one-way glass for ten minutes before even considering my entrance. I could tell he hated the room. I could tell he was losing composure with every passing minute. I left him alone with his thoughts for as long as I could.

Finally, I entered and sat down in the only other chair. A small table separated us. He noticed my injuries, but he didn't mention them.

"Nick, what is this? They won't tell me what's happening."

"Earlier this evening, I was assaulted." I explained. "I'm fine, thank you for asking, but the man who attacked me stole some documents."

"... What's this got to do with me?"

"The only way that someone could know the location of where I'd be picking up the documents is if they'd hacked into our system in the basement."

"You think I hacked your system?"

"I know you did, but let's not debate that. For some time, British Intelligence has been paying for low-level information from the embassy. I was sent here a year ago to investigate a suspect. My inquiry cleared her and implicated you. You've been watched ever since. They couldn't see at first how you were passing the information, but a runner moves so quickly, it's impossible to keep track of everything."

"I don't have to listen to this."

"We only needed you to be careless once, so we set a trap. We let people believe I had photographs that would incriminate Conrad Dean. They don't. They incriminate you."

I placed the documents on the table. Ed looked at them quickly. There was picture after picture of Ed carrying a package to the passenger side of a black Land Rover.

"I don't understand. This is the package I passed on for you."

"The embassy has no record of any such assignment."

"I delivered that parcel to a lady in a car because you told me to. I kept it quiet because you told me to."

"I don't recall asking you to deliver any packages for me." I lied.

"... I don't believe it. You set me up? ... I want to speak to the Embassy. The car's plates are visible in the photos. We'll trace that car, find the woman who owns it, and then we'll see who people believe."

"That won't be necessary. We already ran a trace on the plates. The car belongs to Adam Lewis. He's an MI5 operative working as liaison to the foreign office and formerly the official aide to Conrad Dean. He's the same agent who assaulted me and stole these pictures. He then passed the photographs to the minister who had them in his possession when he was arrested."

I produced further images for Ed's benefit: Adam Lewis attacking me; Adam Lewis passing the envelope to Conrad Dean; Conrad Dean looking at the photographs; Lewis and Dean led from their car by MI5 agents. All of the photographs were the work of President Dan Jackson.

"They have discrepancies in your personal diary Ed. They have record of meetings with a suspected British agent at your favourite bar. They have eighteen months of correlation between information you've had access to and information the British paid for. You think you tell a better version of events? Ed, no one's listening."

"I want a lawyer."

"We've appointed one. She'll meet you at the airport when you get back."

"Get back?"

"You're on a plane in 30 minutes."

Kit, Todd, Maggie, Dan and Ben collected their personal possessions from the basement. No one spoke, but every now and again, one of them would look at another and exchange smiles.

The presidents were the first to leave. As Maggie passed Todd, she slipped him a piece of paper with her phone number. Todd placed it in his jacket pocket and picked up his bag. He threw it over his shoulder, approached Kit and shook his colleague's hand.

"It was good to meet you Todd." Kit said.

"It was good to meet you too."

"I bet you've never served your country like this before. "

Todd produced one of his trademark grins.

"If all assignments were this fun, I'd serve my country more often."

I've flown out of Heathrow airport on four prior occasions. On all of those instances, I was escorted through secure hallways and hidden tunnels by embassy security to expedite my route through the airport and speed my departure. As I walked through its busiest corridors, I realized that I'd never walked down them before.

It was the first time I'd flown home without an armed escort and it felt strange. Part of me missed the attention. Fortunately for me, as I passed the shops and the crowds, Leah was waiting for me.

"I missed you at The Old House and Kit told me where to find you."

"Here to make sure I leave?"

"No. I wanted to thank you for my birthday present."

"Did you like it?"

"It was perfect."

I'd finally closed the case whose inconclusive status had left her under unfair, persistent suspicion. My apology was late, but I'd finally delivered it properly.

"Can I ask you a question?" she whispered as we approached my flight's gate. "I never worked out why Silas or Zack would send you here."

"It's a secret."

"Still keeping secrets? Then, let me guess. I think you promised Silas evidence against Ed Williams and the end of Conrad Dean's political career. He cleared your transfer on the condition that you kept it unofficial. How did I do?"

"It wouldn't be appropriate for me to discuss a confidential matter."

"But I can't figure out what you offered Zack Bristow. He wouldn't clear you for those assignments, not even unofficially. You don't have anything to offer him."

"There was one thing he wanted."

Leah's eyes widened as she reached her answer.

"You resigned?"

"I retired, effective next week. They let me go on medical grounds."

"I don't believe it. ... Tell me you didn't do this for me."

"I did it for you, but I also did it for Kit and for Silas and for some other people. There were some things I needed to put right. Hopefully, I've done that."

"What will you do?"

"I don't know." I admitted. "I need to see my doctor for a final check-up and some referrals. I'm planning to spend a few months in Italy with an old colleague who's interested in my recent project work. After that? ... I'm keeping my options open. Is it true that John Rum was reassigned?"

"It wouldn't be appropriate for me to discuss a confidential matter." Leah replied.

"Then, let me guess. ... Yeah, it's true. ... Maybe that's why I don't know what's next for me. Maybe I'm waiting to see where you go."

I waited patiently for her to reply.

"I've been posted to Washington." she told me. "I'll be there from October."

"I know. I bribed one of your assistants four days ago."

"You'll never change, will you? But maybe that's OK."

She reached into her pocket and pulled out an envelope.

"Kit asked me to give you this."

She handed it to me and kissed me on the cheek, another thank you for her present.

I watched her disappear down the corridor and then opened the envelope. Inside was a printout from an online news site, a clipping that carried a headline of "Hero Cop Gets Something to Cheer About".

The article told the story of a brave policeman, Evan Noah, badly injured in the line of duty. The photograph showed him with friends and family, all dressed in the sports shirts of his favourite team, celebrating a recent cup victory.

I slipped the page into my pocket and walked unaccompanied to the plane.

The Clock Tower

A very short story.

The clock stopped one afternoon and time stopped with it. Nobody knew why.

The philosopher mused that this represented a new age and it diminished all previous thought.

The scientist wondered which long-held laws of physics it disproved.

The attention seeker claimed responsibility. Nobody believed him.

The politician said it was a gift to be used wisely. Everyone agreed, and then disagreed how.

The inventor wanted to design a new future.

The environmentalist wanted to save the planet.

The ambitious philanthropist wanted to save everything.

"Wow." said the clock. "That got serious really fast. I was just messing with you. Do you want me to restart time now?"

Spheres of Creepy Influence

A short story.

The rain clouds rolled in and the shadow they cast left the forest in a melancholy darkness. Dying trees that looked evil in the day twisted into something far worse without the moonlight.

"Did you hear about the attempted murder?" George said.

"Yeah." Jay replied. "That's the third this month. In our neck of the woods too. It would almost be exciting if it wasn't so human."

They gazed through the arch and towards the twisted branches as if they expected another incident while they watched.

"I received some enquiries." George said.

"What kind of enquiries?"

"This area isn't what it used to be. It's getting a reputation with humans as a place to avoid and a reputation in our circles as a place to be."

"You're telling me that some ghosts want to move in." Jay said.

"That's the sum of it, yes."

"How serious are they?"

"The enquiries are serious. The ghosts? Not so much. There are still some high profile locations that have the edge over The Arch: the really old houses; the active graveyards; the old churches that still have an actual church building. Those will always draw your high profile spectres. If we set aside those locations and those ghosts, our corner of the wood is considered a strong tier two base of operations. It's getting attention from, what I consider, strong tier two candidates."

"It's a lot to take in. The Arch has been all ours for a while."

"I feel like we weathered a slower, tougher period." George said. "Now that business is picking up, part of me doesn't want to share."

Jay didn't respond immediately. His mind drifted through all the possible entrants to their established world.

"OK. Who applied?"

"Haydn."

"No. No way." Jay said immediately. "He's embarrassing. He doesn't clear our minimum bar."

"Our bar is really low."

"I know. He doesn't clear it."

"He's still new to this."

"He'd fail a casting call for a haunted house ride. He'd make us look bad and most days we don't need the help. Who else?"

"Patricia."

"No way. She'd make us look even worse."

"Patricia is amazing."

"I know. That's why she'd make us look even worse. She's so far above our minimum bar, she wouldn't see it. She's so far above our bar, I'm not sure how we'd explain the bar's criteria in terms she'd understand. Next."

"Fading Shadow."

Jay rolled his eyes.

"Oh, please. Please don't call him that."

"That's what he likes to be called."

"Exactly. It's a name he gave himself. Every infamous ghost receives a name and the terrified living select it. Self-respecting ghosts don't assign themselves names because they feel like it."

"Give the guy a break. His real name is Algy. Wouldn't you prefer Fading Shadow if your first name was Algy?"

"Rule him out. It wouldn't work."

"It might work."

"Do you want to listen to me complaining about his pseudonym on a daily basis?"

"You're right. It wouldn't work."

"Next."

"Christopher applied and then withdrew his application."

"That's a shame. I like that guy. He's a funny guy."

"He had some concerns."

"What concerns?"

"Mostly with the two of us, and eternity, and the two of us and eternity."

Jay nodded sympathetically.

"Yeah, I get that. You're my best friend, I'm me, and some days I don't want to hang around with us. Can we persuade him?"

"I don't see how."

"That's a pity. He's my favourite candidate so far."

The conversation faltered suddenly. Despite George's efforts, Jay caught it.

"There's another candidate, isn't there?"

"… There is, but you have to promise not to freak out. … It's Gemma."

"… Gemma? My Gemma?"

"You do know that Gemma is not your Gemma, don't you? Her well-established hatred for the term My Gemma should demonstrate clearly that Gemma is not your Gemma."

"Yes, but there are a lot of Gemmas in the world, both living and otherwise. I wanted to establish which of these Gemmas we were discussing."

"Did you hear me ask you not to freak out?"

"I did. That leads me to believe that we're talking about My Gemma. This is unbelievable. Did she attach conditions?"

"Yes, but they mostly involved you not freaking out or using the term My Gemma. She thinks we can make it work if you can keep it together."

Jay sighed and tried to lower his voice's pitch from the elevated note to which it had spontaneously risen.

"She said that? Well, then, I can. … What? I can. I admit that I'm not right now, but that doesn't mean I never will. I strongly believe I have the potential to keep it together and I will demonstrate that ability at some future time that is obviously not right now."

George inspected his friend for any external signs of the inevitable, internal debates.

"… Are you calm now?"

"No, I'm freaking out on the inside instead because I thought it would be less disruptive to the conversation. Was there anyone else?"

"The usual suspects. Eddie wants away from Molly. Molly wants away from Eddie. Nathan wants in, but he wants you out first. Deb said she wants in, but what she really wants is Nathan in so that she can have his spot near the falls. And Will applied because he thought *we* were by the falls. He talked to Deb and got confused; he was too embarrassed to withdraw his application. I've ruled him out along with Molly, Eddie, Nathan, Deb and everyone form the East Wood."

"Who applied from the East Wood?"

"Everyone. They all want out. It's just not as spooky as it used to be."

"So, realistically, it's Haydn, Patricia, Algy, Christopher or Gemma."

"That would be my short list. ... What do you think?"

Jay thought through the candidates, pausing longer on Gemma's name than the others.

"... I'm thinking all of them." Jay said.

"Are you serious?"

"We tell Haydn to improve his game. We tell Patricia to mentor Haydn. We tell Algy that his name is Algy. We tell Gemma that her name is not My Gemma. Then we tell Christopher that he isn't stuck with the two of us, he's stuck with the six of us."

George grinned as he considered the plan's logistics.

"... Wow. That might actually work. ... But seven at The Arch?"

"Seven at The Arch."

"End of an era."

"A good era, but time for a new one."

"Still freaking out?"

"Definitely, but you have to be impressed with how much better I'm hiding it."

"I really am. ... This is a great idea. They're a good group."

"They are."

George looked around at their home. He inspected the failing walls, the arch that gave their home its name and the damaged trees that surrounded them on all sides.

"This was fun while it lasted." George said.

"Everything has to end someday."

"You're right, and sometimes that's OK. ... Yeah. It's OK."

THE END

Acknowledgements

Thank you to everyone who made this possible. As this is the first time I have included an acknowledgements page, I would also like to express my gratitude to the people who assisted with my previous publications. This includes Melissa Symanczyk, Blair Munro, Liesa Evans, Neil Lester, Libby Adams, Kristin Grimstrup, Russ Brown, Barbara Casterton, Bonnie Brightlee, Sue Day and Alex Tassioulas. It also includes Sarah, Daniel, Nick, Wendy, Jon, Chris, and my mum and dad. It also includes everyone that I should have included in this paragraph, but whom I have carelessly forgotten. This is not an exhaustive list and there are many others who deserve a mention.

You are a tremendous group of people. I will never forget that it was all of you who made this possible. Thank you.

Printed in Great Britain
by Amazon